CONNECTIONS

This book was made possible by:
The Missions Division
of The Baptist Convention of NM
PO Box 94485
Albuquerque, NM 87199
Please send them a word of thanks.

CONNECTIONS

Linking people and principles for dynamic church multiplication

Gustavo V. Suárez

Foreword by Claude Cone

Published in the United States by Baxter Press, Friendswood,Texas.
Formatting by Anne McLaughlin, Blue Lake Design, Dickinson, Texas.
Cover design by John Gilmore, Gilmore Marketing, Pearland, Texas.

ISBN: 1-888237-47-3

The versions of the Bible used in this book are the New International Version and the New American Standard Bible.

Printed in Canada

What Leaders Are Saying
About Connections

Gus Suárez has done an enormous favor to every church and minister who is serious about the Great Commission. Church Planting was the pattern of the N.T. church and is to be the strategic movement of the church in our day. Dr. Suárez has skillfully dealt with the issues that are critical to the success in church planting, and additionally has blended his own experience as a Cuban immigrant to America into a strategy for crossing cultures and barriers to such efforts. I commend the book to all who want to effectively plant churches.

Dr. James T. Draper, Jr.
President, LifeWay Christian Resources

To reach the vast number of lost people in the United States requires a mighty movement of God. An intentional massive church-planting movement could very well stimulate such a sweeping spiritual renewal and revival. Only the discovering, developing, and deploying of lay church planters provides sufficient promise for a massive church-planting movement. Gus Suárez has provided strategic counsel for equipping lay people to participate in planting more healthy congregations. His step-by-step guide details specific actions and resources for church planters and sponsoring churches. He has contributed significantly in reducing the intimidation surrounding church planting with *Connections*.

Dr. Jack Kwok
Executive Director and Mission Ohio Team Leader
State Convention of Baptists in Ohio

In this book Gus Suárez has done a masterful job in connecting Biblical principles for committed Christians who desire to obediently get the gospel to every person by the primary methodology of starting healthy reproducing churches. Anything healthy does reproduce! Dr. Suárez' cross-cultural experience and expertise has assisted him in connecting the primary missiological dots for healthy Christians to be intentionally involved in calling out God's people to be on mission to equip and mobilize them as part of church planting movements. This book affirms what many of us in church planting have long believed - church planting is one of the greatest tools of evangelism for impacting a culture if it is intentionally evangelistic in its methodology. Anyone who wants to see their church experience exponential church growth, lead a reproducing church, and learn the practical how-to's must read this book.

Dr. Richard H. Harris
Vice President, North American Mission Board
Church Planting Group

Gus Suárez has always had a passion for planting new churches. That passion comes through on the pages of Connections. Yet, the book is not only about passion--it contains practical and clear steps to guide the church planter. It moves the planter from creating the right environment, to planting a church, and on to church multiplication. It helps church planters to plant for the right reasons and with the right motives. This book will be a gift to church planters who use and apply it.

Dr. Ed Stetzer,
Author, Planting New Churches in a Postmodern Age

Connections is an excellent book on church planting. The book deals with the basics, is easy to read, understand and follow. The book is an excellent resource because it comes from personal experience and leadership positions in church planting. I recommend this book to anyone who is interested in reaching people for Christ. I firmly believe and hope that it will be widely read and used in the days ahead.

Dr. B. Gray Allison
President Emeritus and Professor of Evangelism and Missions
Mid-America Baptist Theological Seminary

Gus Suárez has written from his heart. Church Planting is the passion of his heart. This book will guide you in developing strategies and guidelines for planting healthy new congregations. *Connections* is appropriate as new congregations are planted. Healthy congregations result from good relationships with sponsors and others. I appreciated the spiritual emphasis running through the book. Church Planting must be a spiritual movement if we are to reach untold numbers for Christ.

Dr. Fermin A. Whittaker
Executive Director-Treasurer
California Southern Baptist Convention

Don't let *Connections* sit on your bookshelf and collect dust. Whether you're involved in church planting or longing to see a renewed commitment to multiplication in an established Body, this book will be a trusted resource and practical how-to manual.

Dr. Bob Reccord,
President, North American Mission Board

Nothing can compare to the energy and enthusiasm of a new church start. Nothing will drive a church leader to his knees and keep him there like a new church start. Nothing has potential to advance the Kingdom like church planting. That is why I am so enthusiastic about Gus Suárez's book, *Connections*. This comprehensive book flows from practical experience, is passionate about God's global redemptive purposes, and will help any congregation plant a church — this year! We will be using and sharing it widely in our church planting network.

Dr. Sam Shaw
Senior Pastor
Germantown Baptist Church

To my parents Lino and María Luisa Suárez.
Thank you for modeling for me,
Love, Faithfulness, Perseverance and Integrity.

Table of Contents

Acknowledgements

I thank my God in all my remembrance of you (Phil. 1:3).

It is not possible to write a book without assistance from friends. I will forever be grateful to those who made suggestions and provided encouragement along this magnificent journey.

I give many thanks to the church planting team that works closely with me. Some have been with me for a longer period of time than others. It was in one of our earlier meetings where the idea for this book was born. Daniel Rupp and Frank Shope have helped with comments, suggestions and encouragement throughout. David Putman and David Terry from the North American Mission Board helped me think through some issues that led to the principles taught in the book.

Many thanks to Benjamin Bedford and Carolyn Laughlin who took the time to read the manuscript. Each examined the documents from different points of view. Benjamin examined the manuscript from a missiological position. Carolyn, on the other hand, examined the text for clarity of thought and grammar. Each brings with them a wealth of experience in their respective fields.

Many thanks to Pat Springle from Baxter Press for his constant help throughout the entire process of writing this book. Pat provided not only professional help, but also many practical suggestions that helped make writing this book more enjoyable.

Many thanks to Cricket Pairett, my administrative assistant, for her numerous excellent suggestions and support. She gave many hours to help make this book what it is today. Claude Cone has always provided support and encouragement to this project. I am blessed to be able to serve alongside such a godly man.

Many thanks to my wonderful family for putting up with me during the time it took to write this book. My wonderful wife, Diana, showed patience during the journey, although she often asked when she could have her dinner table back again. Phillip and Matthew, you are both precious gifts that God gave us.

Finally, many thanks to my Lord for having provided the experiences over the last twenty-four years of ministry, which have enriched my life. It is these "connections," which link people together, that have transformed and shaped my life and ministry.

Foreword

The Apostle Paul was a church planter. Of the thirteen letters of Paul, nine fall into the category of what J.B. Phillips called "Letters to young churches." These were newly-founded churches whose members were quite recent and inexperienced converts to Christianity. Most of these churches had been birthed by Paul as he traveled his world sharing the gospel. The majority of the members had been converted to Christianity through Paul's powerful presentation of the gospel. The churches Paul established were always on his mind and in his heart. You can feel the burden of the great church planter when he writes, "Besides everything else, I face daily the pressure of my concern for all the churches" (II Cor. 11:28 NIV). Paul planted churches, and he constantly worked to mature them for his Savior, Jesus Christ.

Gus Suarez is a church planter. He worked in New York planting churches, and he served as a catalytic missionary in Maryland with his primary responsibility being church planting. In New Mexico he has served both as Language Missions Director and as director of the Missions Division of the Baptist Convention of New Mexico. I have watched Gus Suarez for over a decade, and his passion is to start New Testament churches that reach people for Jesus Christ and become strong, self-supporting bodies of believers that will start more churches and reach more people. Be certain that the author of this book has been on the front line of church starting and continues to lead in planting new churches.

This book could well be titled Church Planting 101. About everything relating to church planting is discussed. It is critical that a church plant have the right beginning.

Gus Suarez has laid out the necessary preparations for the success of a new church. The communication between sponsors and the new church must be clear and honest. I know there must be something missing concerning the beginning of a new church, but you will have to agree it is hard to find. This would be an excellent textbook or required reading for any seminary class on church planting. If you or your church are considering a new church plant, please read this book carefully and follow it step by step for maximum success.

You who hold this book in your hands are fortunate. To enable a new church start to begin correctly and avoid dozens of heartaches is a blessing of God. Dr. Suarez has placed in your hands years of knowledge and guidelines to be used in spreading the Kingdom of God through new bodies of believers. Read this book carefully, practice the truths presented diligently and go forward by prayerfully planting new churches.

Dr. Claude Cone
Executive Director
Baptist Convention of New Mexico
Albuquerque, New Mexico

Preface

So Paul stood in the midst of the Areopagus and said, "Men of Athens, I observe that you are very religious in all respects. For while I was passing through and examining the objects of your worship, I also found an altar with this inscription, 'to an unknown God.'" Therefore what you worship in ignorance, this I proclaim to you (Acts 17:22-23).

There are several reasons why I am writing this book about church planting. First, there is a need worldwide to reach the lost with the gospel of Jesus Christ. When you compare churches to population ratio in your area of ministry, you will probably notice a greater growth in the population than in the number of churches. In addition, the people moving into the area are more cosmopolitan than they were in past years. Second, there is a passion within me that wants to share church planting principles and practices so that you also may be part of the church planting efforts in the Kingdom of God. Third, I have had twenty-four years of experience in church planting. My spiritual life, in essence, has been primarily in the area of church planting. In Memphis, Tennessee, I was part of a new church planting experience. In Buffalo and Dunkirk, New York, I was blessed by starting two churches which still continue to experience growth. In Maryland, I served as the Language Catalytic Missionary for the Baptist Convention of Maryland/Delaware. In that capacity, I worked with Language/Culture leaders in developing leadership and starting new congregations among Hispanics and other language groups. Since 1992, I have served with the Baptist Convention of New Mexico in two different capacities. As Language Missions Director, my responsibilities were to discover, train and mobilize leadership for the harvest. Since 1997, I have served as the Director of the Mission/Ministries Division. In that capacity, I direct the overall ministries of the division in the area of women's ministries and mission education, volunteers, language missionaries, disaster relief and church planting. These years of ministry have taken me both to the East and West coast, as well as to rural and urban areas. Fourth, this book is unique in that (a) it gives very detailed biblical reasons for church planting (b) it ties the biblical reasons with the sociological and missiological reasons for church planting (c) it encourages you, the reader, to gradually put together a church planting plan and (d) it includes thirteen intentional and progressive lessons that can be taught in 45-60 minute weekly segments. You may download these lessons by previously obtaining a password. (See information at the end of this section).

A few years ago, my family and I had the privilege of visiting Thailand. As we flew from Los Angeles to Bangkok, I had many hours to reflect about my native country, Cuba, the reason for my existence and how God had taken my life and molded it according to His will. As I stepped out of the plane in Bangkok, I was in the midst of a new country, new culture and a new language. I began to take mental notes as I experienced the sights and sounds of the city on my way to the hotel. I was impressed with the many motorcycles weaving in and out of the city traffic; the friendliness of the people; the humidity of that evening in mid July; and the many temples that adorned the city. But the one thing that most impacted my life, as I walked the streets of the populous city of Bangkok, was the faithfulness of the people to

Buddha. I vividly remember watching people stop to worship at an altar on the sidewalk of a busy street. I thought how these people are very faithful to a dead god while our people seldom find time to worship the living God. That visit left an impression on my mind of the significant need to start churches to reach all types of peoples everywhere with the gospel of Jesus Christ.

The United States reflects the other side of the same coin. The world is coming to America and each group brings its own language, culture and religion. We are a nation of many nations. God, in His infinite wisdom, is bringing the world to our doorstep. The question for the Church today is: "What are we doing to take the gospel to a lost world?"

This is a book about extending the Kingdom of God through the start of healthy reproducible congregations. It is a book about encouraging you to be part of the solution. As for me, I want to be part of the solution! I want to reach all kinds of people by starting different types of new congregations.

I am writing this book primarily for those serving on church staffs and lay people all over the world that are asking the same question, "What am I doing to take the gospel to a lost world?" It is my desire to place in your hands tools and principles that can enable you to be a successful church planter. Connections is about linking people and principles for dynamic church multiplication.

The book is divided into six sections. Section one sets the foundation for creating a healthy environment. The premise is that only spiritually healthy individuals can start healthy reproducible congregations. Part of this foundation is built on the reasons why we need new churches. It is then further strengthened by the biblical, sociological and missiological reasons for church planting.

One key word for this section is "communication." The church planting team and partner churches must be able to communicate that church planting is essential in extending the Kingdom of God.

The second section gives you practical ways to identify those whom God has called to church planting. A common objection to church planting is "we cannot find church planters." The fact is that all the resources you need for church planting are found in the harvest. One key word that identifies this section is "relationships."

The third section explores methods of equipping. The key word to describe this section is "nurture." This section presents very practical and useful ideas about evangelism, relationships, small groups and the role of partner churches. Please note that relational skills, as well as the effectiveness of reaching out to new people, are factors in the growth of small groups. The fourth section takes the church planting team and starts to mobilize more people in the starting of a healthy reproducible congregation. This section leads you to create a church planting partnership, to understand the culture of the contextual environment in which you are working, to know your target area and ministry focus group, and to create a positive image through cultivating events and the development of the core group.

The fifth section is planting. The key word is "celebration." I want to clearly communicate to the readers that church planting ought to be a time of celebration. This section deals with five of six stages of congregational development. These are: conception, development, birth, growth and maturity.

The sixth section will deal with the last stage of congregational development, that of, multiplication. This section will present models of multiplying congregations using both biblical and modern-day examples. It will paint the picture of the American mosaic and some strategies to break cultural barriers in order to multiply. The key elements of an indigenous congregation and some of the common objections to church planting will be discussed. Finally, this section will present you with a challenge to rise up and start a new church. "Reproduction" is the key word for this section.

Pastor, I want to challenge you to guide your local congregation to start a new healthy, reproducible congregation this year. Use this book to lead your people through the thirteen-week study.* Lay people, I want to challenge you to accept this invitation to be involved in a new church planting effort. Let me suggest only some ideas: prayer walking, opening your home to a Bible study group, gathering demographic data, leading an evangelism team, visitation team, children's games, fellowship director or participant, greeter, prayer warrior, media person for the new congregation, outreach director. Can you think of other ministry opportunities?

In the introduction, I want to take you back in time to share my pilgrimage to genuine freedom and how God prepared my life for the ministry He called me to do today. He will do the same with your life. My question to you today is, are you willing to make your life totally available to the Lordship of Christ? (Jn. 15:16)

Gustavo V. Suárez
Albuquerque, New Mexico
July, 2003

*To obtain a password to download the thirteen lessons and PowerPoint contact GSuarez403@aol.com

Introduction
My Pilgrimage to Freedom

So if the Son makes you free, you will be free indeed (Jn. 8:36).

God uses circumstances of life to mold His servants for ministry. Many times, not understanding, we ask the question, "Why do bad things happen to good people?" As I look back on my pilgrimage, I see a God who was molding me for a ministry He would give me years later, among peoples of many different nations.

January 1959 started as a year of hope and new beginnings for the people of Cuba. Fidel Castro's forces caused dictator Fulgencio Batista to leave the country. Castro represented freedom from years of oppression. Yet, that freedom was short lived, since in December of 1961 he announced that Cuba would become a Socialist nation.

INDOCTRINATION

I do not remember much about my kindergarten years. One thing I do remember is that day when the teacher asked us to close our eyes and placed a piece of candy in each student's little hand. She asked the class, "Who gave you the candy?" "God gave us the candy," I replied. She proceeded to give us a lecture that God did not exist and that the candy was given to us by Castro. This presented a conflict of values. I had been taught since early in my life the existence of God, and now school was teaching me that God does not exist. I was also taught that if anyone in the family said anything against Castro, it was my duty to report them to the communist party. Well, it did not take me long before I put that to the test. As a young boy, I was not happy that my parents would not allow me to do something I wanted to do. One day at a distance I saw a "pionero,"[1] whom I approached and told that my parents did not like Castro. He came with me to the house and talked to my parents. Soon after their conversation began, I saw both my parents and the young man laughing, and I knew right then I was in serious trouble. This was confirmed after the young pionero left, and my father gave me a lecture and proper punishment.

The next few years my father would normally ask me everyday, "What did you learn in school today?" He told me recently that he had wanted to make sure that I was not being taught any communist propaganda. He had to make the decision as to whether he would leave Cuba to provide a better future for his children. His daily questions to me were only one factor he considered in finding the answer. Things did not improve, and by 1962 he decided, at the risk of being apprehended himself, to take me out of school. That last year we lived in Cuba, my dad was my teacher.

INITIAL SEPARATION

My father considered sending my sister and me out of Cuba in 1961. That was the year of the Bay of Pigs Invasion. President Kennedy ordered air support for the Cuban exiles that were attacking Cuba from their base in Nicaragua. Kennedy's inexperienced cabinet recommended that he retract the promised air support, as the Cuban fighters were at mid sea. That allowed Castro's forces to dominate, capture and kill members of the 2506th Brigade. My parents made the decision to send my sister to Canada since she was the oldest. This was the first time that I felt the sting of communism in my life. My parents protected me from the initial food rationing. But now they could not hide the fact that my only sister had to leave the country, in search of political freedom, because of communism. That was a definite change, not only for her, but for me as well.

PREPARATION TO LEAVE CUBA

My parents applied for permission for the remaining three of us to leave the country. Despite my young age at the time, there are some lasting impressions that are part of my life and have undoubtedly been a factor in molding it. I remember the piano that adorned our living room. My mother made the comment that she wanted to give the piano to a family friend. For a few days, a friend of the family parked his van in our garage. The last day we put the piano in the van and moved it to our friend's home. A few days later, the lady responsible for spying in our particular block saw that the piano was missing. She came to our door and told my mother she had twenty-four hours to return the piano and place it in the same place it used to be. We went back to our friend's home and brought back the piano.

Part of the requirements to leave the country was the government's inventory of all your possessions. Representatives of the government would come to your home and count every fork, knife, glass, plate, your clothes, etc. Immediately before permission to leave the country was granted, a second inventory was taken. The idea was to make sure that the first and second counts would match. If they did not, you would have to replace the missing item.

My father received a telegram one afternoon informing him that he was to leave the country early the following morning. Even though my parents and I had applied to leave together, the telegram was addressed only to my father. This was the government's way of discouraging people from leaving the country. They believed that if they were able to split the family, they might change their minds. His initial reaction was that he would not leave my mother and me in Cuba. My father's friends encouraged him to leave the country because I was approaching the age of nine years old, at which time I would become part of the "pioneros," making it almost impossible to leave the Island. "If you do not leave now, you are not going to be able to leave," they told my father.

POLITICAL FREEDOM

My father left Cuba in March 1963, to start a new life in Panama. Now my family was split once more. My sister was in Canada and my father was in Panama. In the meantime, my mother and I continued to wait for the Cuban government to give us permission to leave the country. Government representatives came to my home again to inventory our belongings. Finally my mother and I received authorization to leave Cuba in September 1963. We left with the clothes we were wearing and one additional change of clothes. My parents had to leave our home, car, retirement and everything else they owned to the communist government. We flew to Panama where we were reunited with my father. A few months later my sister moved from Canada to join us. Once again our family was together. I completed my third grade during the three months I lived in Panama. My family then moved to Nicaragua where I studied English at the American-Nicaraguan School. My sister got married during our time in Nicaragua and then moved to Maryland, where she presently lives. Those years were days of learning about new cultures, new people and new environments.

In 1967, I moved to Virginia where I attended the Staunton Military Academy for six years. During those six years, I visited my parents in Nicaragua, Colombia and Chile. I believe with all my heart that this was not an accident, but a divine plan of God to develop and prepare my life for a future ministry that He would provide. As I visited these countries, I was able to understand the culture and language of the people.

A QUESTION LEADING TO SPIRITUAL FREEDOM

After graduation from the military school, I attended Bridgewater College in Virginia for two years and then transferred to the University of Maryland. While a student at Maryland, I worked in a local department store. A friend of mine asked me one day, "Do you believe in God?" I was somewhat disappointed in that question. "Of course I believe in God. Who made you? Who made me? Who made the stars and everything in the world? Of course I believe in God." I answered. My friend calmly said to me, "Don't get upset, the Bible tells us that the devil also believes and trembles." When I heard that statement, I realized that I believed, but not enough to tremble. My friend recommended I read the Gospel of John. I started reading it and was not far into the third chapter when I clearly saw that God wanted a relationship and not a religion. That day, January 11, 1978, I surrendered my life to Jesus Christ. That day, I started to enjoy spiritual freedom!

GOD PREPARES THE PERSON

Shortly after my conversion, I learned that many of the students involved in Campus Crusade for Christ at the University of Maryland had been praying for my salvation. As I learned to take my first spiritual steps, Campus Crusade for Christ and the College and Career group of my church took the time to disciple me.

Having been called to ministry by the Lord, I made preparations to attend seminary. While at the seminary, the Lord clearly revealed some life changing truths. I wanted to go to a Spanish speaking country as a missionary. One day, as I attended one of my mission classes, I learned that the guidelines would not allow me to go to any Spanish speaking country.[2] I went home that day very defeated and disappointed. I shed many tears that evening and asked God, "Why?" That night God unmistakably communicated this, "Instead of going to minister to one Spanish country, I will bring the world to you."

God used all the circumstances of my life; separation from family, life under communism and leaving my country and friends for unknown places. God also used the different countries I visited in Central and South America to help prepare me for the future ministry He would give me. Today, I minister not only among English-speaking people, but people of different countries in the world. The Lord, indeed, is bringing the world to the United States.

I am so glad that God looks beyond our imperfections and sees our possibilities. You, too, can be used in a significant way for the Lord. Perhaps, as you read these sentences, you are going through challenging times in your life. Perhaps you are feeling overwhelmed and ready to surrender to the enemy. Wait! Look at His promise, "I will never desert you, nor will I ever forsake you" (Heb 13:5) and ". . .I am with you always, even to the end of the age" (Mt. 28:20). Do not look at the impossible, but keep your eyes on Him who can make all things possible.

Like the apostle Paul, "I thank Christ Jesus our Lord, who has strengthened me, because He considered me faithful, putting me into service" (1Tim. 1:12).

SECTION

one

Creating a Healthy Environment

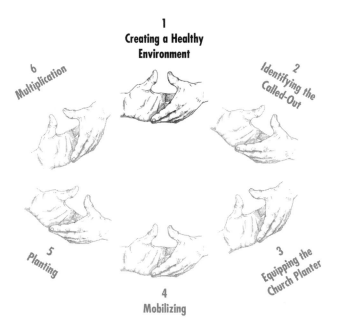

1
Creating a Healthy Environment

6
Multiplication

2
Identifying the Called-Out

5
Planting

3
Equipping the Church Planter

4
Mobilizing

Only spiritually healthy people can start healthy churches. Therefore, creating healthy environments is important if we are interested in starting healthy reproducible congregations. A key word that summarizes this section is "communication." Creating healthy environments deals, to a great extent, with how well one communicates the fact that church planting is extending the Kingdom of God. In this section I will address spiritual check-ups, the joyous task of church planting, practical reasons for church planting, and biblical, sociological and missiological reasons for church planting.

CHAPTER *1* Spiritual
Check-Up

*But the fruit of the Spirit is love, joy, peace, patience, kindness,
goodness, faithfulness, gentleness, self-control; against such
things there is no law (Gal. 5:22-23).*

piritual check-up time!!! "Who me? You don't
understand that my entire life revolves around
ministry." "I love what I do for the Lord. I know I am a
workaholic but after all everything I do is for the ministry." Have you heard someone say something similar?
Perhaps you recognize this statement as a description of
your lifestyle. Maybe you are part of the twenty percent
of the people in your church who do the work of the other
eighty percent. Maybe you are at the point in your life
where you are close to burnout. Stop and do a spiritual
check-up now!

This book is about church planting. The premise is
that only spiritually healthy people can start healthy
churches. "Not by might nor by power, but by My Spirit"
(Zech. 4:6). The foundation for any church planting effort
is an uncompromising commitment to the lordship of
Jesus Christ. This commitment starts when a person calls
out to God. "Whoever will call on the name of the Lord
will be saved" (Rom. 10:13). Everyone who is saved is
gifted for ministry through the church. However, each
person is at a different stage of spiritual maturity. Paul

referred to some in Corinth as "men of flesh and infants in Christ." For that reason "I gave you milk to drink, not solid food; for you were not yet able to receive it" (1 Cor. 3:2).

It is the commitment to the lordship of Christ that is evidenced when Christians "press on toward the goal for the prize of the upward call of God in Christ Jesus" (Phil. 3:14). It is critical that you understand that God has called you to a particular ministry. Unless you are called to your particular ministry, you sometimes will find the pressures and frustrations of your work overwhelming. You can have good intentions and yet run empty if you are pursuing a ministry to which you are not called.

Perhaps you were like me. I was so excited when I started driving that I neglected to keep my eyes on the fuel gauge. As I was leaving work one day, my car came to a sudden stop in the middle of traffic. I knew what to do; I just failed to monitor my fuel. Many people in ministry today fail to keep their eyes on indicators of their spiritual health—the spiritual gauges. These spiritual "gauges" monitor four areas: spiritual, physical, emotional and family health.

Robert was a pastor in a nearby church. One day he and his wife, Janice, came to visit me. Their expressions indicated they were under a lot of pressure. They shared with me their struggles with people in the church, including a specific problem with the lay leadership. There was a group of leaders who seemed to want to control every move Robert made.

In spite of their hurt, Robert and Janice spoke with their usual grace. However, I heard some pessimism and hurt in their voices. During our conversation, I identified some warning signs of their spiritual emptiness. Robert demonstrated personal frustration when he said, "I never finish what I start."

Underlying the entire conversation was Robert's real question: "Is there another place for me to serve?" When stressed, it is human nature to respond with one of two attitudes: fight or flight. Running, however, often is not the best solution to problems. Robert and Janice had reached the point of fight or flight. They were empty in their spiritual, physical, emotional and family lives.

I shared with a church this idea of monitoring our gauges, especially in the midst of being busy serving the Lord. After the service a young woman came to me and said, "I am completely empty."

I have had many similar experiences with both clergy and laity. In each case, the physical, emotional, spiritual and family issues are just symptoms of an underlying problem. Spiritual disconnection is at the heart of the problem. When an individual gets spiritually disconnected from the Lord, everything else spirals downward. Pressure is felt from every side, setting in motion an attempt by individuals to take care of things that normally would have been turned over to God. Physical and emotional fatigue begins to take control, resulting in illness, weariness and lack of focus. Jesus reminded us of the importance of abiding in Him. "Abide in Me and I in you. As the branch cannot bear fruit unless it abides in the vine, so neither can you unless you abide in Me" (Jn. 15:4).

Maybe you think this will never happen to you. Well, think again! No one is immune to the effects of spiritual, physical, emotional, or family emptiness. Let me remind you of three men who experienced a state of hopelessness.

When Moses was leading the Israelites from Egypt to Cannan, he encountered their desire to return to Egypt. "We remember the fish which we used to eat free in Egypt, the cucumbers and the melons and the leeks and the onions and the garlic, but now our appetite is gone there is nothing at all to look at except this manna" (Num. 11:5-6). Sometimes we get so comfortable with the way things are that we are unaware that God wants to provide so much more. The Israelites stopped focusing on what God had in store for them and resumed focusing on themselves. The Israelites were spiritually disconnected. They could not rejoice in the manna because they were too busy thinking of the past. Moses' dilemma was seen in his prayer to God. "Was it I who conceived all this people? Was it I who brought them forth, that you should say to me, 'Carry them in your bosom as a nurse carries a nursing infant, to the land which you swore to their fathers'? Where am I to get meat to give to all this people? For they weep before me, saying, 'Give us meat that we may eat'" (Num. 11:12-13).

Elijah was another godly man who, in the midst of doing ministry, lost sight of his spiritual health. At Mount Carmel Elijah confronted 450 prophets of Baal. He told them to prepare the altar, choose an ox and cut it up and place it on the wood. But he told them to put no fire under it. Elijah did the same and then challenged the prophets of Baal. He told them to call upon their god while he called upon Yahweh and "the God who answers by fire, He is God" (1 Kg. 18:24). The Baal prophets called on Baal but there was no answer. At noon Elijah told them, "Call out with a loud voice, for he is a god; either he is occupied or gone aside, or is on a journey, or perhaps he is asleep and needs to be awakened" (1 Kg. 18:27). Finally it was Elijah's turn. He called the people around him as he prepared the altar. He then prayed to God and "the fire of the Lord fell and consumed the burnt offering and the wood and the stones and the dust and licked up the water that was in the trench" (1 Kg. 18:38).

What a tremendous victory. When the people saw the altar consumed, they said, "The LORD, He is God; the LORD He is God." God showed His power before the people of Israel. Queen Jezebel wasn't so thrilled at Elijah's encounter with the prophets of Baal. She promised Elijah he would be dead within twenty-four hours.

Elijah had just been a part of an incredible display of God's power, yet he feared for his life and started running. Elijah lost his spiritual direction and suffered physically and emotionally.

1. He ran to Beersheba and left his servant there (1 Kg. 19:3).
2. He went a day's journey and sat down under a juniper tree (1 Kg. 19:4).
3. He requested that he might die (1 Kg. 19:4).
4. He slept under a juniper tree (1 Kg. 19:5).
5. He had a "martyr syndrome" (1 Kg. 19:10).

These are symptoms of someone who felt hopeless despite God's show of superiority at Mount Carmel. One moment Elijah was at the top of the mountain and the next he was afraid and running for his life.

Jonah was another prophet of God who neglected his spiritual health. His life was full of ups and downs. He ran away from the call of God to go to Nineveh. "But Jonah had gone below into the hold of the ship, lain down and fallen asleep" (Jnh. 1:5). Sin has a way of anesthetizing people. Everyone around Jonah was afraid of the strong winds and cried out to their own gods. But the prophet of God was sleeping on the job. The captain, perhaps a pagan, asked Jonah, "How is it that you are sleeping? Get up, call on your god. Perhaps your god will be concerned about us so that we will not perish"

(Jnh. 1:6). The second chapter of Jonah details Jonah's fasting and prayer. Eventually, Jonah was released and ended up preaching a revival in Nineveh. Even though the revival was successful, Jonah got angry with God.

God is good all the time! Look at how God provided for the needs of each person. The Lord said to Moses, "Gather for me seventy men from the elders of Israel, whom you know to be the elders of the people and their officers and bring them to the tent of meeting and let them take their stand there with you....and they shall bear the burden of the people with you, so that you will not bear it all alone" (Num. 11:16-17).

As Elijah rested under a Juniper tree, an angel appeared and gave him bread and water. "He arose and ate and drank and went in the strength of that food forty days and forty nights to Horeb, the mountain of God" (1 Kg. 19:8).

For Jonah, God provided a plant "and it grew up over Jonah to be a shade over his head to deliver him from his discomfort" (Jnh. 4:6).

The spiritual disconnection of these three men of God is seen in their prayers. Moses prayed, "So if You are going to deal thus with me, please kill me at once, if I have found favor in Your sight and do not let me see my wretchedness" (Num. 11:15). Elijah's prayer was similar, "It is enough; now, O Lord, take my life, for I am not better than my fathers" (1 Kg. 19:4). And, Jonah prayed, "Therefore now, O Lord, please take my life from me, for death is better to me than life" (Jnh. 4:3). Can you identify with any of these people? God loves you and He will provide for your every need. He did so with Moses, Elijah, and Jonah, and He is continuously providing for you.

The spiritual health of the church planter is the foundation for the new congregation. A church planter is pressured to visit, build new relationships, work with a core group, be a family person and much more. The spiritual health of the church planter cannot be replaced by anything. The joy of church planting is the spiritual growth of the planter.

REFLECTION

1. Think back to the time when you accepted Jesus as Lord and Savior. Trace your spiritual pilgrimage in terms of growth. Highlight the highs and lows in your pilgrimage. State specific highs and lows and what caused them.

2. In what ministries are you involved through your church? Are you ministering because you want to help or do you feel God specifically called you to that ministry? What are your gifts?

3. Have you experienced, or are you now experiencing, emptiness in your spiritual, emotional, physical or family life? What factors contributed to the situation? How did you feel? What were your thoughts? Where was God? What positive steps did you take to regain your health?

4. Do you feel that you are now spiritually disconnected from God? Are you running from God? If so, how and why?

5. Can you identify with any of the examples of people that were running on empty presented in this chapter? Pray and thank God for His goodness. Write down how He provides for your needs.

The Joyous Task of Church Planting

*All authority has been given to Me in heaven and on earth. Go
therefore and make disciples of all the nations, baptizing them
in the name of the Father and the Son and the Holy Spirit,
teaching them to observe all that I commanded you; and lo, I am
with you always, even to the end of the age (Mt. 28:18-20).*

*H*ave you ever been to the maternity ward of a
hospital? How exciting it is to glance at all of
the newborn babies and rejoice at their births. They wear
little hats to keep their heads warm, their legs and arms
are moving and they are breathing without the help of
their mothers. The umbilical cord has been cut, yet for
many years to come they will need the help and support
of other people such as parents, family, teachers, doctors,
friends, church members and others. This is an excellent
analogy of church planting.

I remember when my wife was expecting our first son.
Very early one morning she said to me, "I think it is time
to go to the hospital." We got in the car and drove to the
hospital in Annapolis, Maryland. I had practiced the
breathing techniques and I was looking forward to my job
as a coach. Soon after our arrival in the hospital, I expected the birth of our son. However, we spent the next six
hours walking up and down the halls of that hospital.
Finally, in the late afternoon, the doctor told us that he did

not think it would be wise to wait any longer. He said, " We need to do a Cesarean section." They gave me disposable surgical attire and I went into the labor and delivery room.

Following the birth of our child, my face was glowing with excitement. I was full of joy. I followed my son everywhere they took him. Finally, as I was joyfully walking down the hall of the hospital, my Italian mother-in-law told me that my pants were ripped in the back! I honestly did not care. My excitement swallowed up any embarrassment I might have felt at that time. Such is the joy of church planting.

Other reasons why church planting brings me great joy are that:

Church planting is kingdom growth
Roland Allen said it best when he said,

> In a little more than ten years St. Paul established the Church in four provinces of the Empire, Galatia, Macedonia, Achaia and Asia. Before AD 47 there were no churches in these provinces; in AD 57 St. Paul could speak as if his work there was done and could plan extensive tours into the far west without anxiety lest the churches which he had founded might perish in his absence for want of his guidance and support.[3]

The need to work together is greater than ever. We live in a time of tremendous multicultural growth. Look around your community and take note of the differences in race, national origin, language and so forth. But, in the midst of the multitude of differences, we must pursue that which we have in common—Christ, the Word and the command to reach the world with the gospel.

Church planting helps fulfill the Great Commission

The Great Commission starts with the words "all authority." Jesus established that He is in control both in heaven and on earth. "God highly exalted Him and bestowed on Him the name which is above every name" (Phil. 2:9).

The word "go" in the Great Commission is best translated "as you are going." This communicates the idea that the Lord expects us to be on the go. When my son was playing soccer, it was amusing to see all the little kids around that soccer ball. The coach would yell, "Bust Out," to communicate to the players to spread out and advance while covering the entire field of play.

In Matthew 8, the Lord demonstrated for us what he meant by "go." The leper came and bowed down before Jesus and said, "Lord, if You are willing, You can make me clean" (Matt. 8:2). Jesus immediately replied, "I am willing; be cleansed" (Matt. 8:3).

As Jesus entered Capernaum, a centurion came to Him and said, "Lord, my servant is lying paralyzed at home, fearfully tormented" (Matt. 8:6). Jesus said, "I will come and heal him" (Matt. 8:8).

As Jesus continued the journey, He entered Peter's home and saw his mother-in-law sick with a fever. Jesus touched her hand and the fever left her. As the crowd began to surround Jesus, He told the disciples to depart to the other side of the sea. He got in the boat and went to sleep. While he slept a great storm arose, and the disciples became so terrified they woke Jesus up and said to Him, "Save us, Lord; we are perishing!" (Matt. 8:25). The winds obeyed His voice, and the sea became perfectly calm.

Just as Jesus was intentional in His going, the church must be intentional in its "going." The Lord is saying, "Bust out and be intentional about reaching the lost with the gospel."

"Make disciples" is the command in the Great Commission. It involves leading people to the Savior, incorporating them into the local church and developing them into learners, followers and ministers who are busy expanding the Kingdom of God.

"All nations" includes all people groups in the world. No people groups are excluded from this command. It is for this reason that all types of churches must be intentionally started in order to reach all the people of the world.

"Baptizing" is the act of obedience on the part of the new believer. It is a public expression of a commitment to the Lordship of Jesus Christ.

"Teaching" speaks of the continued development of the Christian. We never stop learning in the process of becoming more like Jesus.

The Great Commission provides the foundational authority for the mandate, the sending orders to the people of God, the instructions to the followers of Christ, the span of the mandate, the public demonstration of obedience, the equipping methodology and the assurance that God will never leave us.

Church planting is exciting!

It is not only about planting new congregations, but congregations that are healthy and reproducible. It is about the lives that will be transformed, the workers that will be released into the harvest and the new churches that will be planted out of the sponsoring churches. It is about fulfilling the Great Commission.

Church planting is a process

Every church owes her existence to the visionary leadership of a person or a church. Each congregation has the responsibility to communicate its vision and plant new congregations. We are called to reach the lost for Christ and make disciples, but not to maintain new churches. It is a time-consuming process.

Church planting is controversial

Many people are fearful that starting a new church will take members away from their congregations. Others see the many church buildings in a particular neighborhood and make the assumption that new congregations are not needed. These people, for the most part, fail to recognize the growth of the unchurched, coupled with the declining and dying churches, which increases the need for more churches to reach the growing population.

Church planting is rewarding

It is a joy for a church planter and his leadership team to see the birth of new congregations. It is rewarding to see how the new group grows from a core group to a larger group of people. It becomes similar to the birth of a newborn child and the joy experienced by the parents and grandparents. It is a movement from the initial stages of dependency to an independent person now able to reproduce and start new congregations as well.

Church planting is evangelistic

Peter Wagner said, "the single most effective evangelistic methodology under heaven is planting new churches."[4] The relationship between evangelism and church planting cannot be separated without violating the mission of the church. Donald McGavran said, "Increasingly the primary assignment of missions is evangelism: the proclamation of the Good News and assisting in the emergence of churches which, rooted in the soil and with their own leaders, will be witnesses to the Good News."[5] The apostle Paul saw as his primary mission the preaching of the gospel and the establishment of churches.

Church planting is difficult time consuming

It is essential for the planter to spend more time out in the field and less in the office. He needs to make contacts with core group members and with the lost people in the community. It is also healthy for the church planter to share notes with other church planters in that area. It involves time driving to meetings with partner churches and with people interested in the new work.

Unfortunately, pastors of many established churches criticize church planters. They may not understand the innovative approach used by many of the church planters. They feel that what has worked in the past will continue to work today. Perhaps, both the pastor and the church planter need to establish a dialogue to help them better understand each other. Unwarranted criticism can affect the spiritual health of the church planter.

The joy found in church planting, or in any other ministry for that matter, is rooted in your call. During the difficult days, it is the call of God that will sustain you. During my seminary years, I felt that God was calling me to the mission field. In those early years, I felt I could minister in a Spanish speaking country. Everything came unraveled for me in my mission class. The guidelines of that time would prevent me going as a missionary to any Spanish speaking country. "Why? I speak the language and know the culture of the people." I remember shedding lots of tears. But then, the Lord revealed to me that He would send the world to me here in the United States. Now I fully understand what He meant. It is my joy to minister among 19 different Indian pueblos, Navajos, Apaches and over 13 different nationalities among the Hispanics. In addition, I minister to people from Asia, the United States and other countries of the world. God is indeed good all the time! Without understanding God's call, I would have walked away from His perfect plan for my life.

REFLECTION

1. If you are now involved in church planting, think about the aspects of planting that bring you joy. What are the difficulties you face in church planting? Describe how God called you to church planting.

2. If you are not involved in church planting, begin to investigate potential areas where a new church is needed. The denominational office in the area where you live can assist you with necessary information.

3. Who lives around your neighborhood? Walk around the area where you live and pray and observe the people. Are they native to your area? From another state or country? Do they have young or older children? What type of work do they do?

4. Describe your life as a believer. Compare your actions with Jesus' actions in Matthew 8. How do you compare to Jesus in your focus and determination to live up to your calling? In what areas of your life do you need to make changes? List three things you can do this week to regain your focus on your mission.

3 *Practical Reasons for Church Planting*

The harvest is plentiful, but the laborers are few; therefore beseech the Lord of the harvest to send out laborers into His harvest (Luke 10:2).

C hurch planting is spiritual warfare. When one starts a new congregation, he is reclaiming territory that belongs to God, but temporarily was under the control of Satan. Paul Beals reminds us that evangelism in the New Testament never stands alone. Winning the lost to Christ is only the initial step in the church's mission. Believers must be gathered into local churches for edification and service. Planting new congregations is essential to New Testament missions.[6] Therefore, a healthy congregation is one that has as a priority winning the lost, edifying believers and planting new congregations.

THE NEED FOR CHURCH PLANTING

Approximately 95% of the population of Canada is unchurched. It is estimated that only 5% of the population is evangelical. In the United States 50% of the population is unchurched. I believe this is a very conservative figure. According to George Barna only 8% of the US population is evangelical. Among Southern Baptists, 75% of our existing churches are plateaued or declining.

Many churches in North America are closing their doors every year. According to Win Arn, about "3,500 to 4,000 churches die each year."[7] Lyle Schaller said that any large denomination can expect to loose 0.5% of the existing churches every year. That has been our experience in New Mexico among Southern Baptist churches.

North America's growing ethnic populations demand not only new churches, but different types of churches. The total Hispanic population in the United States has surpassed the total African American population. California and New Mexico are the only two states without a racial majority. Nationwide, the population is growing faster than churches are being started.

The Baby Boomer generation demands new types of churches. This is the generation born between 1946 and 1964. They make up a third of the population of the United States. While it is true that the Boomers are, in general, unchurched, a Gallup survey indicated a strong interest in spiritual matters.[8] Boomers interviewed by Jack Sims described their church experience as "boring, irrelevant, or high-pressured."[9] One can conclude that the boomers are not uninterested in church, but they are looking for something different. Malphurs makes an excellent observation when he said that, "the way we 'package' our faith is predominately cultural and subject to change on the part of those who are willing to be flexible in order to reach unchurched lost people."[10]

Generation X or Baby Busters necessitate new church planting methodologies as well. These are the children of the Baby Boomers and, therefore, second generation unchurched people. Whereas a great number of Boomers dropped out of church, the Busters, for the most part, were never in church.

The growth of cults and non-evangelical groups calls for new church starting efforts in North America. An increasing number of people are attracted to Islam and New Age beliefs. Additionally, there are new immigration patterns in North America, with more people coming from areas of the world where Islam, Confucianism, Taoism and Buddhism exist.[11] These cults are winning people who were former churchgoers and others that did not have any prior commitment to a church.

The North American Mission Board reports in its "Strategy for the Church Planting Group," some very interesting facts concerning demographic, psychographic and ecclesiological issues.

Demographic issues:
1. United States   281,422,000
2. Canada   31,000,000

Psychographic issues:
1. United States
    a. Builders (born before 1946)   59,260,437
    b. Boomers (born 1946-1964)   82,826,479
    c. Busters or Generation X
        (born 1965-1976)   39,891,724
    d. Bridgers or Millenial (born 1977-1994)   80,261,468.
    e. Babies (born since 1994)   19,175,798

2. Canada
    a. Builders (born before 1947)   7,457,000
    b. Boomers (born 1947-1966)   9,900,000
    c. Busters or Generation X
        (born 1967-1979)   5,600,000
    d. Baby Boom Echo (born 1980-1995)   6,500,000
    e. Millennium or Net Generation
        (born since 1996)   1,000,000

Ecclesiological issues:
1. North America is an unevangelized continent.[12]
2. The United States of America is today the largest mission field in the world.
3. Between 92 percent and 98 percent of Canadians are unchurched.
4. Evangelical churches have failed to gain an additional two percent of the American population in the past fifty years.
5. Half of the churches in the United States did not add one new member through "conversion growth."
6. North America is the only continent where Christianity is NOT growing.
7. The church to population ratio is declining for every 10,000 Americans.
   a. In 1900 there were 27 churches for every 10,000 Americans
   b. In 1950 there were 17 churches for every 10,000 Americans
   c. In 1996 there were 11 churches for every 10,000 Americans

We indeed face a great challenge. Yet, in New Mexico, only 3.71% of our existing churches are involved in starting new congregations. Among Southern Baptists, the number of established churches that were involved in a new church starting effort was approximately five percent.

THE EXPERIENCE OF CHURCH PLANTING

Our experience in church planting has taught us many things. The church planters, as well as students of the church planting movement, have validated these eight practical lessons. The task before the church is monumental. Churches today are confronting a very different world than that of the 1950s. Today we have an unchurched population that requires different methodologies from the church of the past.

1. Growing populations need new congregations

As population centers continue to experience growth, new congregations are needed. Even in areas where a number of churches already exist, new congregations must be started soon or there will be fewer churches in proportion to the population in the future.

2. Older churches are likely to plateau

Many of the churches in America are either plateaued or declining. The life cycle of the church is similar to that of humans. It starts with birth and ends with death. Somewhere in that pilgrimage, the cycle turns downward and decline begins. Many church growth experts believe that point is reached about the tenth year. Bruce McNicol tells us that, among evangelical churches, those less than three years old baptize ten people for every one hundred members. Churches between three and fifteen years old baptize five for every one hundred members and those beyond fifteen years old baptize three people for every one hundred members.[13] As congregations grow, they tend to become more inwardly focused and become less concerned for the lost.

3. No church can reach everyone

While it is true that a church is for all people, not everyone will go to that church. Every city is made up of people of diverse backgrounds. These people differ in their socio-economic levels, language, culture, music and worship styles. No church can reach and disciple all these different types of people. New congregations are needed to reach the diverse people in particular areas.

4. New churches are more flexible

New churches are able to be more flexible than established churches. New congregations seem to adjust more readily to the community than existing churches do. Established congregations can become slaves to traditions. Meaning to do well, they fail to see the connection between the church and community. When this occurs, it signals the beginning of the downward cycle. For many congregations, maintaining tradition may become more important than reaching people.

5. New churches are more evangelistic

Most new congregations reach and baptize more people than do established congregations. In the state where I serve, this generally has been true. In responding to a question related to the future of denominationalism, Lyle Schaller said, "Southern Baptists made evangelism and church planting the focus of their ministry and the future was bright." He further mentioned that any church or denomination that makes evangelism and church planting their primary tasks will flourish. C. Peter Wagner made a similar assertion when he said, "Without exception, the denominations that are growing are the ones that emphasize the establishment of new churches."[14]

6. New churches encourage established churches

The planting of a new congregation usually motivates established churches. New congregations often are outwardly focused and very intentional in evangelistic efforts. This causes the partner church to reexamine its priorities as a church. Many partner churches have experienced an increase in membership and finances as a result of starting new congregations. Many other established churches that are not involved in new church planting get so energized as they observe the enthusiasm of new congregations, that soon they are seeking a place to start a new congregation.

7. New churches reach new communities

Residents of a new community are generally more receptive to new churches than are those of established communities. One reason for this may be that in new communities, residents have not established relationships. Many are looking for an opportunity to meet new friends and develop new relationships.

8. New churches develop new leadership faster than established churches

As new congregations are started, the number of people that form the core group is small, compared with the membership of an established church. Most of the members of the initial core group are usually highly motivated people. They see a need for reaching more people and building a strong church. Therefore, this group of people generally is motivated to leadership roles. On the other hand, the pastor of a new congregation is granted credibility and trust up front. In the case of an established church, the pastor must earn the credibility and trust of the people. The difference is that in the new church, the people are joining the pastor while in the established church the pastor is joining the people. Many established churches lose ministry focus while "honeymooning" with a new pastor.

REFLECTION

1. Make a vertical line on a sheet of paper. On the left side write "feelings." On the right side "God is telling me." As you read the section on the "Need for Church Planting," what were your feelings? Write them on the left side. What is God telling you about what you read? Write them on the right side.

2. In the city in which you live, are there churches that once were flourishing and are now struggling? What do you think happened? Are there churches that are experiencing tremendous growth? What are they doing differently?

3. Do you know a language/culture group in your area that does not have any churches ministering to them? What can be done? Could you start a Bible study among that group?

4. Find someone this week who does not go to church. After establishing a friendly conversation, ask why he/she does not go to any church? Could it be that the churches are not meeting his/her needs?

5. After studying the demographic, psychographic and ecclesiological issues, do you think new churches are needed? Write five reasons we need new churches.

6. Determine the unchurched population of the area where you want to start a church. Follow these steps:

    a. What is the total number of churches in that community? (All faiths)
    b. What is the seating capacity of each church?
    c. Multiply that number by 2. (number of services)
    d. Add the numbers to get a total.
    e. Subtract this number from the total population of the area.

Example:
a. 7 churches
b. 100; 200; 500; 1000; 200; 100; and 300
c. 200; 400; 1000; 2000; 400; 200; and 600
d. 4,800
e. total pop. 80,000 – 4,800 = 75,200 number of unchurched

 *Biblical Reasons for Church Planting*

For the Son of Man has come to seek and to save that which was lost (Luke 19:10).

America is a nation of immigrants. Churches in the United States have a tremendous opportunity to reach people of various cultures. The world is coming to America. We live in a global village. Yet, a lack of understanding of the real meaning of sponsorship (partner churches) in church planting could rob churches of their opportunities to minister cross-culturally. Another consequence of the lack of understanding is the absence of indigenous leadership and contextualized training. There are four theological pillars that are biblical foundations for church planting.

THE LOSTNESS OF HUMANKIND

The greatest motivation a Christian has for witnessing is the fact that everyone without Christ is already condemned and bound for eternity in hell. The reason for the existence of the church is to proclaim the gospel and to provide for the spiritual nurture of the people of God. T. V. Farris correctly observes:

Salvation would be nothing but a nebulous and elusive philosophical concept were it not for the savage reality of the human sin problem. The very notion of spiritual deliverance is inextricably connected with the issue of human moral depravity and condemnation.[15]

Unless the church believes the truth of the total depravity of humankind, it will not be motivated to reach out, much less take time to sponsor a new congregation. Sin needs to be understood on the evidence of Scripture rather than defined by sinful humanity. The Bible defines sin as missing the mark. The Hebrew word *chatha* and the Greek word ἁμαρτάνω point to the fact that all wrongdoing is a failure or a coming short of the aim which God intended all His children to reach.[16] Both of these words picture "an archer aiming an arrow at a target, representing God's will, character and glory. The arrow comes short—misses the mark—of the glory of God."[17] Other words such as iniquity, transgression, wickedness, rebellion and crookedness, also describe sin.[18] In the beginning, God's voice broke the cosmic silence in order to create the earth. The Bible reminds humanity over and over, "God saw that it was good." The crown of God's creation was when "God created man in his own image, in the image of God he created him; male and female he created them" (Gen. 1:27).

Adam and Eve decided to yield to temptation rather than obey God. Therefore, the serpent's deadly venom of rebellion fell upon humankind, thus introducing sin into the created world. As a result, "the eyes of both of them were opened and they knew that they were naked; and they sewed fig leaves together and made themselves loin coverings" (Gen. 3:7). Because of sin, lost humanity disturbed the harmonious relationship of humankind with God and with each other. Kenneth Matthews points to this event as "part of the sad deception that man and woman who wanted so much to be 'like God,' rather than obtaining the stature of deity, are afraid even to commune with him."[19]

Lost humanity blames others for its mistakes. Adam answered God's question by saying it was "the woman whom You gave to me" (Gen. 3:12). Eve similarly responded to God by passing the blame to the serpent: "the serpent deceived me and I ate" (Gen. 3:13). One can readily notice that lost humanity does not take responsibility for its mistakes, even when God expects accountability. "From the very beginning, man and woman were held individually accountable for their personal conduct. No manipulation of conscience can remove the guilt of the guilty."[20]

Lost humanity already is condemned to hell—an eternal place of separation from God. Humanity is condemned because no one is righteous before God (Rom. 3:10); all have sinned and fall short of hitting the bull's eye (Rom. 3:23); the wages of sin is death—eternal separation from God (Rom. 6:23); humanity is separated from Christ and without God (Eph. 2:12).

Perhaps the saddest commentary on lost humanity is that it is the object of God's wrath (Eph. 2:3), which ultimately leads to hopelessness. John Eadie mentions that there is "no hope of any blessing which cheers and comforts, no hope of any good either to satisfy them here, or to yield them eternal happiness. . . . Their future was a night without a star."[21]

Three parables that describe human lostness are found in Luke 15. Jesus used the term "lost" on numerous occasions. *Apollumi* (lost) has "the strong meaning to utterly destroy. It is translated in various places as to be ruined or rendered useless, to kill or destroy, to be wasted and useless and to perish."[22] The parable shows the progression. "It was serious to lose a sheep, worse to lose money and worst to lose a son."[23] Two ideas presented in the parable are that of something which was lost and the rejoicing that comes when it is found. "For the Son of Man has come to seek and to save that which was lost" (Luke 19:10). The sheep, coin and lost son all represent unregenerate people. "The sheep strayed from the fold and was lost in the wilderness; the coin was lost in the house and lost, not by its own volition, but through the carelessness or inattentiveness of the owner."[24] The lost son wasted his life in useless things. Three principal teachings from this parable are: (1) the lost are away from the father in a far country; (2) the lost are wasted in uselessness; and, (3) the lost are in grave danger of destruction and ruin. The theme for lost humanity continues to be one of separation, uselessness and death.

These principles are further illustrated by the apostle Paul's description of the lostness of humankind in Romans 3:10-18. Hershel H. Hobbs explained Paul's discourse of Romans 3:10-18 as follows: (1) Paul looked at sin through the eyes of a philosopher (Romans 3:10-12), (2) Paul looked at sin through the eyes of a physician (Romans 3:13-14) and (3) Paul looked at sin through the eyes of a historian (Romans 3:15-18).[25]

The passage above reveals the need for humanity to be rescued from its alienation from the Savior. Salvation originates in God. Humanity's inherent desire is to do that which is not pleasing to God. A lack of righteousness before God leads to a lack of understanding and a turning away from God. Humanity is indeed worthless (Rom. 3:10-12). The throat, the tongue, the lips and the mouth are used for sinful acts. "We tend to take the gift and place it in the service of our own sinful nature. The throat of the unrighteous is an open grave."[26] The unrighteous man's instinct is to kill; therefore, his life is characterized by the shedding of blood, personal ruin and misery. Lost people do not know God and, consequently, do not know the peace of God (Rom. 3:15-18).

Humanity is indeed separated from God and already condemned. This makes God's mandate to "Go therefore and make disciples of all nations" (Matt. 28:19) all the more important. Redeemed humanity is responsible before God to share the gospel. Therefore, the body of Christ must work together to accomplish this God-given task.

RELATIONSHIPS OF HUMANKIND

No person can exist alone. He must be able to interact with others. Life certainly would be very simple if humans were able to associate only with those people who think and act like them. However, that is not the case. It may be by the providence of God that humans relate to different types of people. We become better persons as each of us relates to others.

For a Christian, the matter of loving God becomes important as one thinks of interpersonal relationships. "Love the LORD your God with all your heart and with all your soul and with all your might" (Deut. 6:5). This must be the starting point of any healthy relationship. The Levitical law called for humankind to "love your neighbor as yourself" (Lev.19:18). The apostle John, speaking of love, told us that if anyone says, "'I love God,' yet hates his brother, he is a liar; for the one who does not love his brother, whom he has seen, cannot love God whom he has not seen" (1 John 4: 20). Pondering the above verses, a reasonable question would be: "Can a faithful, committed Christian hate a particular person?" Again, a Christian's relationship to God must be right.

That is, he needs to be filled continually with the Spirit. For it is out of a right relationship that love, a fruit of the Spirit, is nourished. As one becomes immersed in his relationship with God, a natural outcome is a right and healthy relationship with those around us who are different. God intends to work through people. Therefore, relationships between people must be established. Some of these relationships will be positive while others will be a struggle. The primary fact is that relationships are very important in our lives.

Guy Greenfield in his book, *We Need Each Other,* writes about a relational theology.[27] The fact that God sent Jesus Christ to reconcile sinners to Himself and to bring together a group of believers into a fellowship is based on relationships.[28] As believers assimilate into the life of a local church, further relationships will develop and, in some cases, deteriorate. The Greek word *sun* is translated as "along with, in company with, together with, or with." It is used as a prepositional phrase 123 times.[29] This same preposition is used in Acts 2:44 describing Christians believing together, ministering together (Acts 2:45), worshiping together (Acts 2:46), growing together (Acts 2:47), rejoicing and weeping together (Rom. 12:15), fellow heirs, members and partakers together (Eph. 3:6), fellow citizens (Eph. 2:19), fellow workers (1 Cor. 3:9) and fellow soldiers (Phil. 2:25), just to name a few.[30]

The creation of the world was born in the heart of God because He wanted a relationship with humanity. Genesis 1:26 communicates some things concerning the relationship between God and mankind. First, humankind was created in the image of God. Some define the image as the intellect. Others define it as the ability to make decisions. Many have defined it as something spiritual in human nature. In other words, the spirit or soul of our Lord is in us. However, these efforts have limited the meaning of the "image of God." Bert Dominy, like Greenfield, talks about a relational theology. He defines "image of God" as the capacity for a personal relationship with God.[31] The capacity to obey God separated us from the rest of creation. Yes, it includes reason and the ability to make decisions, but is much more comprehensive.

The idea of a relational image is seen also in that, "male and female He created them" (Gen. 1:27). This verse reveals that humankind was created to have a personal relationship with God. But we must relate to other human beings as well. Human relations are both individual and social.

Being created in God's image presents us with our responsibility for the care of the earth. We are to use the resources of the earth in a wise and creative way.[32] Humankind was made, according to Psalm 8, "a little lower than God." It was in God's eternal plan to allow humanity, made in his image, to rule over the created beings. "Rule over the fish of the sea and over the birds of the sky and over every living thing that moves on the earth" (Gen. 1:28).

Healthy people care for one another. God is known as the Great Provider. In Genesis 22:1-14, God provided a sacrificial lamb for Abraham. The apostle Paul talked about a God who will "provide for all my needs" (Phil. 4:19). The idea of caring for one another is found in many passages of Scripture.[33] Examples of these are:

1. Encouragement – "Therefore encourage one another and build up one another" (1 Thess. 5:11).
2. Unity – "May the God who gives perseverance and encouragement grant you to be of the same mind with one another according to Christ Jesus. . ." (Rom. 15:5).

3. Acceptance – "Accept one another, just as Christ also accepted us to the glory of God" (Rom. 15:7).
4. Instruction – "Competent to instruct one another" (Rom. 15:14b).
5. Mutual Submission – "Submit to one another out of reverence for Christ" (Eph. 5:21).

A different side of relationships from what we have been discussing, is that of strained relationships. Many of the struggles result from a goal to gain personal desires, while ignoring the needs of the other person. Jay Adams stated that human relationships are a three-way, not a two-way affair.[34] It always goes back to a personal relationship with God. People are different in many ways. They want different things, have different motives, purposes, aims, values, needs, drive, impulses and urges.[35] The struggles among people who have no relationship or a strained relationship with God are seen throughout Scripture. Genesis 2 and 3 present the ideas of fellowship (Gen. 2:23-25), destruction of the fellowship (Gen. 3:1-6), guilt (Gen. 3:7-8), accountability (Gen 3:9-13), punishment (Gen 3:14-20), God showing His love (Gen 3:21) and Exile (Gen. 3:22-24). Other examples are: Saul's jealousy and attempted murder of David (1 Sam. 18:1-11), the attitude of the Pharoah of Egypt in dealing with Moses (Ex. 6-11) and associating with sexually immoral people (1 Cor. 5:9).

No one can change the fact that we are all different. Neither can anyone change our basic personality types. But, as individuals, we can look at our personality type and study our strengths and weaknesses in order to better relate to those around us.

THE DIVERSITY OF HUMANKIND

Cultural pluralism is a reality in the United States because we are a nation of immigrants and a tapestry of cultures, traditions and languages. Many states have a high percentage of ethnics. New Mexico is the state with the highest percentage of Hispanics. Biblically, the case can be made that God created people in His image but they developed cultural differences as Abel and Cain did.[36]

Diversity is seen from the first pages of Scripture. There is a wide diversity of occupations. Abel was a shepherd, while his brother Cain worked the soil (Gen. 4:2). Tubal-Cain forged all kinds of tools out of bronze and iron (Gen. 4:22). Some were carpenters and builders (2 Kgs. 12:11) and others musicians (2 Kgs. 3:15). Shipbuilding was another of the occupations mentioned in the Scriptures (2 Chr. 20:36). Peter and others were fishermen (Luke 5:1-7). Luke was a physician (Col. 4:14).

Diversity is also seen in the educational level of the people. Gamaliel, a Pharisee, was a teacher of the law (Acts 5:34) and Paul was his student (Acts 22:3). On the other hand, Peter and John were unschooled and ordinary men (Acts 4:13).

Linguistic differences are also highlighted in the Scriptures. The first biblical list of people groups is presented in Genesis 10. These people were "separated into their lands, every one according to his language, according to their families, into their nations" (Gen. 10:5). Genesis 11:7 describes how God confused their language, so that they would not understand one another's speech. Some scholars have observed this diversity in languages as punishment because of humanity's sinful rebellion against God.[37] Acts 2:5-11 mentions a list of fifteen language groups. According to C. Peter Wagner, it is possible that many more groups were present at this time, since the Jewish Talmud indicates there were 70 nations in the Jewish dispersion.[38]

Some biblical examples showing ministry among a diverse people are: Phillip's witness to the Ethiopian eunuch (Acts 8:26-28); Cornelius and Peter responding to the same call of God despite two different cultural backgrounds (Acts 10); and Jesus ministering to the Samaritan woman (John 4).

Diversity, if not properly understood, can easily lead to cultural conflicts. The choosing of seven men to serve tables came as cultural conflict arose between the Grecian Jews (Ἑλληνιστῶ ν) and the Hebraic Jews (Acts 6:1-6). The former were Greek-speaking Jews, while the latter were Jews who spoke the native Aramaic dialect of Jerusalem.[39] Polhill adds that "there is no reason to picture a breach or separation in the total Christian community— only the sort of 'distancing' created by natural linguistic and cultural differences."[40] The Jerusalem council's (Acts 15) central missiological issue dealt with contextualizing the gospel among a new group of believers.

Many, ignoring culture, expect the body of Christ to be united into one cultural tradition. Unity does not mean uniformity. Should a non-Hispanic meeting someone from Mexico encourage him to retain his Spanish or to give it up? Or do we help the individual do what he wants, whatever it is, going along with him both linguistically and ecclesiastically?[41] Ralph Winter mentions that some verses might allow one to make the assumption that God will ultimately unite all believers into one new people consisting of one new cultural tradition. He adds that there seems to be far more references on the other side.[42]

Three passages that normally are presented as arguments for the position of one culture in Christ are: "There is neither Jew nor Greek, there is neither slave nor free man, there is neither male nor female; for you are all one in Christ Jesus" (Gal. 3:28).

> But now in Christ Jesus you who formerly were far off have been brought near by the blood of Christ. For He Himself is our peace, who made both groups into one and broke down the barrier of the dividing wall, by abolishing in His flesh the enmity, which is the law of commandments contained in ordinances, so that in Himself He might make the two into one new man, thus establishing peace and might reconcile them both in one body to God through the cross, by it having put to death the enmity (Eph. 2:13-16).

> And have put on the new self, who is being renewed to a true knowledge according to the image of the One who created him-a renewal in which there is no distinction between the Greek and Jew, circumcised and uncircumcised, barbarian, Scythian, slave and freeman, but Christ is all and in all (Col. 3:10-11).

Many scholars underscore the idea of unity in Christ to the extent of eliminating ethnicity, economic power and gender in their interpretation of Galatians 3:28. Such seems to be the opinion of Nicole, Jamieson, Fauset, Brown and others. It is my view that a proper interpretation of these verses would be to understand them in terms of our position in Christ. A.T. Robertson, making reference to Galatians 3:28, supports the idea of position in Christ by saying, "This radical statement marks out the path along which Christianity was to come in the sphere (en) and spirit and power of Christ."[43] He adds,

"Candour compels one to confess that this goal has not yet been fully attained. But we are on the road and there is no hope on any way than on 'the Jesus road.'"[44] R. C. H. Lenski's observation is that "these and similar distinctions and differences are wiped out as to your spiritual standing."[45]

Timothy George asks, "Does Galatians 3:28 really teach that being 'in Christ' eliminates the three distinctions mentioned in the text? It is clear from the larger corpus of Paul's writings that it does not. Paul himself did not cease to be a Jew once he became a Christian."[46] To ignore the differences in gender would be to violate Scripture. Before the fall of man, God created man in His own image ". . .male and female he created them" (Gen. 1:27). If one follows the thought of no gender to its logical conclusion, he will find unisex, which is a violation of Scripture.

Colossians 3:11 is very similar to the Galatians 3:28 passage. In this verse, one also observes division on the bases of race, religion, social and economic class. Lenski mentions:

> Some misunderstand Paul's thought and quote various passages to show that we are all one in Christ Jesus, that all national, social and other differences are wiped out, that 'brother' should be substituted for all of them. . . Here he says that the new man alone counts, that Christ is everything in all and every way, that all else is nothing in religion.[47]

The new man (νέοξ) is a new creation in the sense that he did not exist before.[48] The present participle (ἀνακαινούμενον) "is being renewed," shows a process of continuous renewal. καινοξ, which is part of the previous word, communicates the idea of quality.[49] The two aorist participles, "having put off" (ἀπεκδυσάμευοι) and "having put on" (ευδυσάμευοι), denote a decisive momentary act while the present participle, "is being renewed," denotes continuousness and iteration.[50]

The "dividing wall of hostility" (Eph. 2:14) presents the idea of prejudice of one group for another. It also speaks of the regulations of the Mosaic Law towards these people.[51] The wall communicates the idea of alienation and separation. Paul was accused of taking Trophimus across this wall (Acts 21:28).

In summary, these three verses have been used against language congregations because it segregates people. But, I like to point out that this is no different than the age-graded Sunday school; it exists in order to provide for specific needs of the people.

THE PLAN OF GOD TO REACH HUMANKIND

The mission of the church was born in the heart of God. It is God's plan to reach people through people.

From the beginning, God's redemptive activity in history seems invariably to be expressed through persons and a people. Today, persons are the followers of Jesus Christ and the people are the church and the mission of the church is to glorify God through Christ. But the average believer and the average church often fail to sense their unique role. . . .[52]

This is a real, but sad statement about the people of God on earth. It is this reality that has led me to pursue writing this book about healthy reproducible congregations. Therefore, the local church becomes central to our discussion in this book. I will define church, for the purpose of this book, as a group of called and baptized believers that gathers together regularly for evangelism, ministry, fellowship, worship and prayer (Acts 2:42-47). The church is not a building, but the people of God. Peter described "the strangers in the world" (1 Pet. 1:1) as follows:

> But you are a chosen race, a royal priesthood, a holy nation, a people for God's own possession, so that you may proclaim the excellencies of Him who has called you out of darkness into His marvelous light; for you once were not a people, but now you are the people of God; you had not received mercy, but now you have received mercy (1 Pet. 2:9-10).

The work of the church is only done through the "people of God." ". . .God's people are a missionary people and the basic unit through whom God works is the local church. Anything done in the name of missions, which erodes the place of the local church, is counter to God's design."[53]

The church must be a caring community. This care must drive the church to reach the lost. But, beyond reaching the lost, the church must take responsibility to teach those it wins to Christ. "The idea that growth is both needed and expected is one of the New Testament's central themes."[54] A very great need in our churches is for true discipleship. Consequently, it is not surprising that many sponsor churches do not develop their mission churches. Lavonn Brown, speaking on Matthew 28:19-20, says: "The implication is that new Christians are underdeveloped and need to be taught how to live as Christians. Regeneration is a new birth; discipleship is a process of growth."[55]

A caring church believes that every Christian is a minister. "Therefore, we are ambassadors for Christ. . . "(2 Cor. 5:20) and "God's fellow workers" (1 Cor. 3:9). Christians are described as a "holy priesthood" (1 Pet. 2:5). "The priesthood was not abolished by the reformation. It was expanded beyond a clerical elite to the whole people of God. Priesthood is not something we reject or delegate. It is a ministry in which the whole church shares."[56]

The church must be a serving community. διάκουος, a noun, means a servant, attendant, minister or deacon. In Mark 10:43 Jesus said, ". . .whoever wishes to become great among you shall be your servant." Another verse, using the same Greek word, tells us that He "made us adequate as servants of a new covenant. . ." (2 Cor. 3:6). The words "fellow worker" are used in 1 Thessalonians 3:2 in reference to Timothy. διάκουέω, a verb, has a comparable meaning to the above word. It is used as a servant, to serve, wait upon and minister. It is used in Matthew 8:15 as someone who is ministering to the guest.[57] In Acts 6:2, it is used with the idea of one that supplies the necessities of life.

The noun διάκουος presents the idea of being, while the verb διάκουέω presents the idea of doing. Ministry is a combination of both being and doing. Many Scriptures speak of the people of God serving others (Deut. 10:12; Matt. 4:10; 6:24; 10:24-25; 20:28; 25:31-36; Eph. 6:7; Phil. 2:5-11). Service is worshiping God (Gen. 12:7-8), providing for the needs of others (Acts 6), reaching out to people in need of salvation (Isa. 49:8-9), using human instruments to provide for the needs of the people (Isa. 49:10), comforting one another in times of trouble (2 Cor. 1:4; 7:6), listening and proclaiming (Matt. 10:26-30), learning, teaching, fellowshipping, relationship building and prayer (Acts 2:42), sharing with others (Acts 2:44). Jesus, our supreme example, said that "the Son of Man did not come to be served, but to serve and to give His life a ransom for many" (Matt. 28:20). We, the people of God, are servants.

The playing field for this service is a multicultural world. Both Matthew 28:19-20, "all nations," and Acts 1:8, "Jerusalem, Judea and Samaria," suggest the sharing of the gospel across linguistic and cultural barriers.

REFLECTION
1. What are the four theological pillars mentioned in this chapter? How do they relate to church planting? Write it down. Can you think of other Biblical reasons for church planting?

2. List three reasons theology is important in church planting.

3. Read Galatians 3:28; Ephesians 2:13-16 and Colossians 3:10-11. What do these passages tell you about cross-cultural ministries?

4. Do you agree with the interpretation of Galatians 3:28 made by A.T. Robertson, Lenski and others? What applications can you make to your present ministry?

5 Sociological Issues in Church Planting

And he said to them, "You yourselves know how unlawful it is
for a man who is a Jew to associate with a foreigner or to visit
him; and yet God has shown me that I should not call any man
unholy or unclean (Acts 10:28).

*T*he next two chapters will explore various issues
from the disciplines of sociology and missiology. I
am mindful that some of the issues are controversial;
however, it is essential that anyone in a position of sponsorship or that of church planter consider a new
paradigm. Please note that, when we talk about cross-cultural partnerships, we are also talking about ministering
among different generations as well.

The relationship between the partner church and the
new church plant does not take place in a vacuum.
Whatever happens within this partnership will ultimately affect the potential of the new work. One sociological
reason to consider is the relationship of people and culture. "Efforts to plant churches in a given culture are
affected by the people's concept of leadership, respect or
lack of respect for age, patterns of decision-making and
ideas about such things as worship and music."[58]
Sherwood Lingenfelter and Marvin Mayers suggest that
persons called to minister in a foreign setting must
become acutely aware of the cultural differences they will

encounter. One cannot effectively minister to others unless he culturally identifies with them. Failing to identify with a people group will increase the possibilities for cross-cultural conflict.[59] Edward Pentecost, referring to people in cross-cultural ministries, emphasizes that one "must first live among the people to win the right to be heard if he is going to penetrate into the 'inner sanctum' of their life experiences."[60] A sincere desire to understand the other person's culture is needed in cross-cultural partnerships. Historically, missionaries have denounced many cultural practices as evil by transplanting their culture as the only acceptable way.[61] Paul Hiebert further explains that missionaries, "have equated the Good News with their own cultural background. This has led them to condemn most native customs and to impose their own customs on converts."[62] The gospel calls all culture to change. Not everything in any culture is bad. Nevertheless, because cultures are created by people, they become stained by sinful practices. Among these are slavery, apartheid, oppression, exploitation and war. "A truly indigenous theology must not only affirm the positive values of the culture in which it is formulated, but it must also challenge those aspects which express the demonic and dehumanizing forces of evil."[63] Pentecost describes the high respect I have for culture in the following statement: "To destroy culture is to destroy a way of life or design of living. To divest man of his culture without offering a functional substitute is to place man into a vacuum where he finds only frustration"[64] (see Chart 2 at the end of the chapter).

A second sociological issue is that people look at the same thing from different perspectives. When a statement is presented to another person, it goes through a filter that interprets the statement according to the way he perceives the world, thinks, expresses ideas, acts, interacts, channels the message and decides (see Chart 3 at the end of the chapter).[65] Recently a Navajo lady expressed that much of the Sunday school literature does not communicate with her culture. She showed me a picture of a beautiful green lawn surrounded by a white picket fence and a little boy watering the grass. She said, "We cannot identify with this picture. We do not have picket fences or beautiful green lawns on the reservation."

Words used in one culture may mean something totally different in another culture (see Chart 4 at the end of the chapter). Thinking patterns of cultures are also different. "In the West, communication follows the logical-linear pattern."[66] Asian and American Indian patterns are similar in that both cultures think in a circular pattern. A thought is expressed, then expanded, then restated and expanded again.

Different cultures make distinctions in how issues are confronted. Some will not plan ahead, while others may take a production and profit approach. Some are very individualistic and others will look for a group consensus. Some cultures put emphasis on the handshake and the touch, while others dislike it. Some are direct and confrontational while others, such as the Japanese culture, place a high premium on manners and on working indirectly to achieve one's purpose.[67] The intent in understanding the culture of all participants involved in cross-cultural partnerships is to enhance communication and reduce the opportunities for conflicts. "When the orientation of a whole culture conflicts with that of the missionary, attempts at cross-cultural communication and ministry may become characterized by hostility and strife."[68]

A third sociological issue is that people assimilate at different rates. Israel Zangwill introduced the idea of the melting pot at the turn of the twentieth century. He describes his idea of "melting pot" as follows:

> East and West, North and South, the palm and the pine, the pole and the equator, the crescent and the cross—how the Great Alchemist melts and fuses them with his purging flame! Here shall they all unite to build the Republic of Man and the Kingdom of God. . . .Peace, peace, to all you unborn millions, fated to fill this giant continent.[69]

It was not the idea of immigrants to be part of the melting pot in total assimilation. Lee sees instead a mosaic harmony of different racial and ethnic groups in the United States. While it is not possible for people to melt totally, as Zangwill and others suggested, it is a fact that people are found at various stages of assimilation.

A study on *Chicano Ethnicity* by Keefe and Padilla concluded that cultural awareness (an individual's knowledge of cultural traits such as language, history, cultural heroes) decreases rapidly between the first and second generation and thereafter continues to decrease steadily until the fourth generation. On the other hand, ethnic loyalty (the preference for one's cultural orientation and ethnic group rather than another) decreases slightly between the first and second generation and thereafter it remains virtually the same.[70] This helps explain why there is an increase in social and ecomonic interaction with Anglo Americans between the first and second generations, even though it tends to be formal, while the more intimate social life within the home and family tends to be ethnically closed.

Chart 1

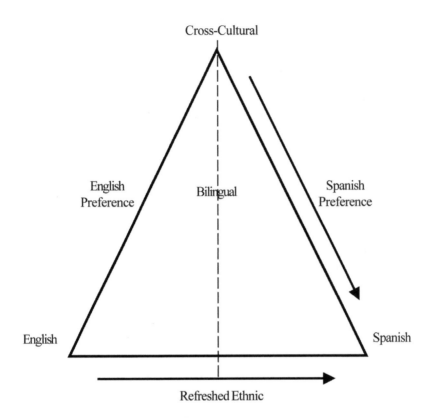

Various models have been presented to show these different stages of assimilation. The previous model is most descriptive of language/culture people in the United States. Although this model will look at Hispanics, it is representative of any language and culture in the United States. As you study the model, note that at either end of the continuum, there are monolingual Hispanics. One speaks only Spanish, while the other speaks only English. The former is true of the new immigrants and the elderly, while the latter reflects many Hispanics in the United States. The other two groups represent people who are bilingual. These two groups are capable of speaking both languages but rely on Spanish or English as their primary language. The Spanish-dominant individual is usually first generation, while the English-dominant is a second or third generation person. Some of these may have some difficulty in expressing themselves in the non-dominant language. In the center of the continuum is found the person who is able to communicate and relate in two languages and cultures with ease. A common misconception is that when a person gets close to assimilation, he will lose the ethnic identity. Numerous studies indicate that acculturation and ethnic identification are, in fact, separate processes.[71] The diagram shows that it is possible for those who have reached the apex of the triangle to try to recapture their ethnic identity. These I call "Refreshed Ethnic." Glazer and Moynihan's classic study of ethnic groups in New York City demonstrates that ethnic identity can remain unchanged or can be strengthened despite virtually complete acculturation.[72]

The lesson one can learn from these models is that many different types of churches are needed in order to reach people of different language/culture and generational groups. People must be given the opportunity to hear the gospel without having to cross linguistic and cultural barriers.

Chart 2

Segments of Culture

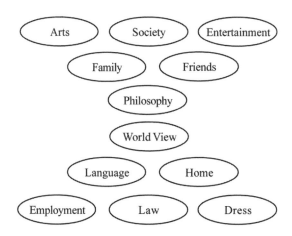

Interrelationships of Culture

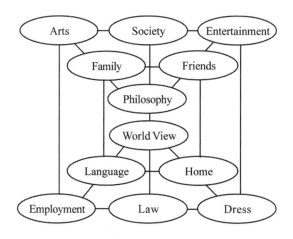

Adapted from Issues in Missiology by Edward C. Pentecost. Copyright 1982 by
Baker Book House Company. Used by permission of Baker Book House Company.

Chart 3

DIMENSIONS OF CROSS-CULTURAL COMMUNICATION

DIMENSIONS OF CROSS-CULTURAL COMMUNICATION

CULTURE X | MICROCULTURE | MACROCULTURE | CULTURE Y

M   World Views - ways of perceiving the world   M

E   Cognitive Processes - ways of thinking   E

S   Linguistic Forms - ways of expressing ideas   S

S   Behavorial Patterns - ways of acting   S

A   Social Structures - ways of interacting   A

G   Media Influence - ways of channeling the message   G

E   Motivational Resources - ways of deciding   E

ENCODES

DECODES

RESPONDENT

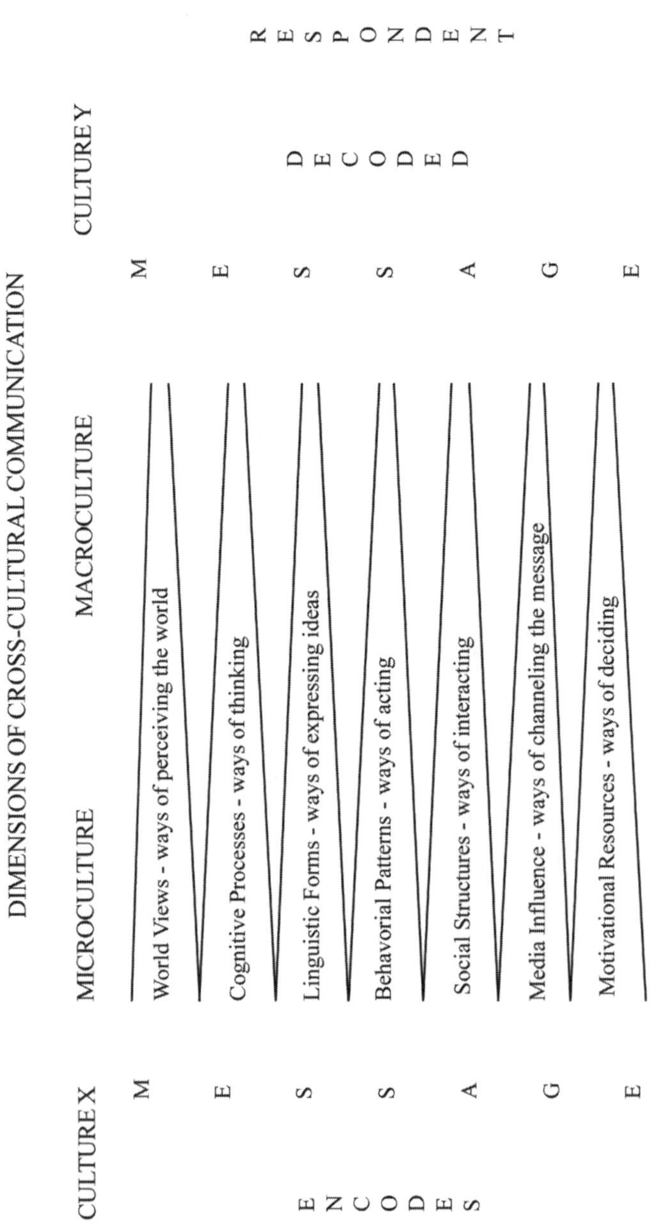

Taken from COMMUNICATING CHRIST CROSS-CULTURALLY - REV ED by DAVID J. HESSELGRAVE. Copyright © 1978, 1991 by David J. Hesselgrave. Used by permission of The Zondervan Corporation.

Chart 4

SAME WORDS WITH DIFFERENT MEANINGS

WORDS	CUBAN	NEW MEXICAN	OTHER COUNTRIES
Ahora	Now, this very moment!		In a little while. Not of such importance.
Ahorita	In a little while. Does not have to be done now.		Now, at this very moment! Immediately!
Guagua	A bus.		To someone from Chile, it means a small baby.
Tortilla	An omelet.	Food made out of corn or flour. It is round.	
Camión	A truck	A bus.	
Tamal	Made out of corn with pork inside.		Made out of bananas and it has vegetables inside. (Puerto Rico)
Sencillo	Something that is simple.	Loose change.	
Menudo	Loose change.	Food.	
Sancocho	Leftover food given to pigs		Typical dish in some countries.
Almuerzo	Lunchtime.	Breakfast.	

REFLECTION

1. What are the three sociological issues mentioned in chapter five?

2. Why do you think relationship is so vital between partner churches?

3. Why is the understanding of culture or generational differences so important in planting new churches?

4. Can you think of a conflict that came about as a misunderstanding of cultures? What happened? What could have been done differently?

5. Do you agree that "different types of churches are needed to reach different types of people?" What types of churches are needed in your area?

Missiological Issues in Church Planting

So then those who were scattered because of the persecution that occurred in connection with Stephen made their way to Phoenicia and Cyprus and Antioch, speaking the word to no one except to Jews alone. But there were some of them, men of Cyprus and Cyrene, who came to Antioch and began speaking to the Greeks also, preaching the Lord Jesus. And the hand of the Lord was with them and a large number who believed turned to the Lord (Acts 11:19-21).

*T*he homogeneous unit principle is defined by McGavran and Arn as "a group of people who all have some characteristic in common and feel they 'belong.'"[73] It is an attempt to address the socio-cultural needs of people. However, I feel more comfortable with Ebbie Smith's idea of a homogeneous strategy rather than Peter Wagner's homogeneous principle. A principle is absolute, while a strategy is a means to an end.[74] The Homogeneous Unit strategy (hereafter referred to as HU) has been used by many to rationalize racism. In fact, race is only one of many elements that constitutes a HU. "Factors such as occupation, education, age, special interests and background draw people into homogeneous units."[75] In a missions conference where my wife and I spoke, I was accused of segregating people by ethnicity. If one looks at our present society, he will find that the

American Medical Association, the American Association for Retired Persons, etc., exist to address specific needs of those people. Is this segregation? Is the age-graded Sunday school segregating people? No, they are addressing the socio-cultural needs of specific groups of people just as the HU strategy attempts to do.

Some strengths of the HU are worth mentioning: First, the HU strategy recognizes linguistic patterns and cultural identity. Second, HU strategy promotes effective evangelism because the gospel is communicated to a group of like mind and interest. Third, group evangelism results in that the group itself recognizes growth, thus leadership and maturity emerge.[76] Fourth, HU strategy facilitates the communication of the gospel without creating unnecessary barriers. Fifth, HU strategy promotes diversity as a "positive force for producing richness, variety and mutual appreciation among Christians."[77]

There are some dangers that should be mentioned concerning the HU. First, it can be used to support separation between people. Statements such as, "Let them go to their churches and stay out of ours," display an unbiblical attitude. Second, HU strategy may "lead to isolated, non-missionary churches that consider their entire task that of ministering to their kind of people."[78] Miles writes in support of the HU strategy:

The growth agent, local church and denomination which can learn to mine the gold which is in the homogeneous unit principle, without sacrificing the pearl of great price which is the gospel, will experience fantastic church growth. America is a mosaic of homogeneous units. Almost every community is a mosaic of such units.[79]

The HU strategy is only one strategy that has been used effectively in reaching language/culture people in the United States.

Beside the HU strategy, a second missiological issue to consider is practical training of the laity. So often it is said, "we need to start churches and develop our leaders," yet no one takes the time to teach others how to do it. A partner church must care to develop the tremendous potential among the laity of the new church. The church should be a training school. "The multiplication of ministry through the empowering of the laity is a powerful dynamic for church growth."[80] Training, in order to be effective, should be contextualized. That is, it needs to be relevant to the people to whom one is trying to minister. The implication for the partner church is that they not only need to have an understanding of the culture, but a genuine desire to minister to people that are different from them.

A third missiological issue is the development of a profile of the people to be reached. Demographic data will reveal important information, giving the partner and new church a portrait of the people in that area. Information such as age, education, employment, housing and additional facts will allow partner churches and the new work to provide for the specific needs of the people. Without this information, a church may attempt to reach young people in an area where many senior adults live. Some places where one can access demographical information are: (a) Government Printing Office in Washington, D.C.; (b) Census bureau through the internet; (c) Universities with printed and computer copies of the material that can be used on site; (d) North American Mission Board or Lifeway Church Resources; and, (e) county, city and state planning offices.

A fourth important missiological issue for us to consider is the type of personnel placed in each field. Do we need a full-time or bivocational minister? Most churches want a full-time minister, but often cannot afford the salary and benefits. Population density is one factor that helps determine the type of ministry and personnel needed. If a small percentage of your target group lives in the area, it would be unrealistic to expect the new work to grow to a point they can support a full-time minister. A bivocational pastor should be deployed to that area. Other factors to consider are the education, income and stability of the people.

Some advantages of having a bivocational pastor are: (a) He gives an example of Christian calling integrated with secular vocation; (b) a bivocational pastor is able to identify with the people at his secular work; (c) a bivocational pastor is more readily aware of the power of the laity in order to multiply his ministry; and, (d) the church can put more financial resources in the mission field rather than personnel. Some disadvantages of a bivocational pastor are: (a) he cannot dedicate full-time to the church; (b) a bivocational pastor may feel isolated and frustrated; (c) a bivocational pastor may lack Christian fellowship; and, (d) a bivocational pastor may not feel accountable to the local church for his work.[81]

REFLECTION

1. Study Acts 11:19-21. Use various commentaries. Do you see examples of cross-cultural evangelism? Explain.

— Do you see evangelism among the same people group? Explain.

— What does this say to you today?

2. What are some elements that contribute to the homogeneous strategy? Are most people in your congregation fairly similar with regards to these elements?

3. What are some strengths of the Homogeneous Unit?

4. What are some dangers of the Homogeneous Unit?

5. Why do you think many churches are not empowering the laity? How does this affect the growth of the individual?

6. What is the importance of demographics in church planting?

7. Visualize your area of ministry. What type of personnel for church planting will you need?

Creating a Healthy Environment

Practical steps I can take

1. Form a "new work" team. The team should be elected by the church.

2. Pray regularly as a team. Mail prayer requests regularly to church members.

3. Develop a "new work" area on the church's bulletin board.

4. Share about the joy of church planting with the church. This can be done in creative ways. Use dramas, small videos, testimonies, bulletin board or a combination of these.

5. Share practical reasons why a new church is needed. You may use some of the same techniques as described in this book.

6. As a team take some time to study the biblical, sociological and missiological reasons for church planting

7. Remember to have fun in what you are doing!

S E C T I O N
two
Identifying the Called-out

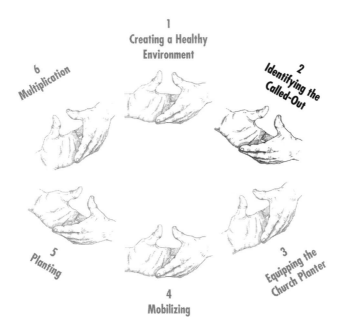

1
Creating a Healthy Environment

6
Multiplication

2
Identifying the Called-Out

5
Planting

3
Equipping the Church Planter

4
Mobilizing

Probably the most important step in a healthy reproducible congregation is getting the right person to start the church. I believe God has provided all the resources needed, including the called-out person. An essential question one must ask is, "Am I a church planter?" In addition, churches interested in starting new works must know what personnel are needed, how to mobilize the laity and how they can develop church planting leaders through existing churches.

7 *Am I a Church Planter?*

*I will give thanks to you, for I am fearfully and
Wonderfully made . . .(Psalm 139:14).*

an Lewis came to visit me one early morning to talk about his desire to start a new church. He was serving as the minister of youth of one of the larger churches in the city. He was determined and enthusiastic. Dan, without any doubt, was a man with a plan. He had an entrepreneurial spirit about him but, more important-ly, Dan was a man in tune with the Lord. He said to me that day, "God is calling me to start a church." We began a process of assessment with Dan and his wife, Tracy and discovered that indeed there was great potential for suc-cess. Following God's lead, Dan resigned from his church and began the joyous task of planting a new church. On that first day there were over 200 people in attendance. That was February 1997. Today, that growing church, SoulRio, averages six hundred in three services. Dan is not a successful church planter because of numbers. He is doing extraordinary things because God called this young, energetic man to plant a church and he obeyed. There was a call from God and obedience by a man with a passion to reach people for Christ. Today, Dan helps mentor new church planters.

The three key people in the church planting team are the church planter, the spouse and the mentor. The church planter may also be a single person, in which case, the planter and the mentor will be a team. Every team needs to function well together. Paul makes the comparison of the body of Christ to the human body.

The Bible tells us that ". . .we are to grow up in all aspects into Him who is the head, even Christ, from whom the whole body, being fitted and held together by what every joint supplies, according to the proper working of each individual part, causes the growth of the body for the building up of itself in love" (Eph. 4:15-16).

Over the years, I have seen planters who have a passion to start new churches but without spousal support. Over time, the church planter grows frustrated and exhausted. I also have seen the reverse, an energetic spouse who encourages the other partner to pursue church planting only to end in frustration for both.

I remember graduating from seminary and moving with my wife to Buffalo, New York to serve as pastor/church planter in that area. In the beginning, there were some very difficult days, but there were also some great days. Our ministry was full of joy. It was during these years when my passion for church planting flourished. What was the difference between my experience and that of other church planters? It was a call from God, a supportive spouse and a mentor that made the difference. I often think of those who started church planting alongside me, but never finished the race. They experienced failure in their ministry. Some were able to bounce back but others never did. What can an organization do to prevent this from happening? In today's sophisticated world, we have tools to help the church planting team. The partners involved in church planting discover the strengths and weakness of people in the team. The church planter's assessment is such a tool.

I suggest using a combination of tools such as personal assessment as well as the behavioral interview process. When someone shows interest in church planting, we give them a few personal assessment instruments to complete at his or her own pace. If the instruments indicate that a person has potential in the area of church planting, a behavioral assessment interview is scheduled for the planter and spouse.

There are several values to the combination of personal and interview assessment:

1. The initial personal assessment can be done in privacy between the planter and spouse.

2. They could determine, after taking the initial personal assessment, that church planting is not for them at this time.

3. The personal assessment is cost effective to the organization and the planter in terms of both time and money since no travel or lodging is involved.

4. The combination of personal assessment and interview process gives a very descriptive picture of how the planter is more likely to act based on past behavior.

5. It is a way for the planter to know more about himself or herself. God made each of us very unique. The assessment process helps us discover that uniqueness.

6. It is a way to translate the knowledge of individual spiritual and personal uniqueness to accentuate strengths and to overcome weaknesses.

7. To the funding partners, assessments provides a process to both mobilize only those that fit the criteria for church planting and to be good stewards of God's resources.

The combination assessments will give a very accurate portrait as it relates to four basic areas of ministry.

PASSION

The apostle Paul had a passion to evangelize the lost, edify the believer, establish churches and exalt Christ. The significant part of his passion was the preaching of the gospel. This passionate desire to proclaim the gospel was the instrument God used in Paul's life to accomplish the evangelizing, edifying, establishing and the exaltation of God. He was "set apart for the gospel of God" (Rom. 1:1). It was this passion that lead him to say, ". . .for woe is me if I do not preach the gospel. . ."(1 Co. 9:16).

Passion is a strong or intense feeling that moves one to action. It deals with your emotions. It makes you feel motivated. It might be realized in your desire to win the lost, teach, preach, protect the unborn, feed the hungry, defend the helpless and provide various needs for the poor. Passion shows persistence despite encountering obstacles along the way. It is not a passing fad, but a real burning fire in the planter's life.

This passion develops out of felt needs. Bill Bright had a passion to reach the students on university campuses; Billy Graham and Luis Palau have a passion for the lost; and out of his own experience in prison, Chuck Colson has a passion for those people who are incarcerated.

SPIRITUAL GIFTS

Unfortunately, many church leaders are more concerned with matching a name to a particular position than they are to matching a person's gifts to a specific place for ministry. The difference between these two approaches can be the difference between joy and frustration in ministry.

Spiritual gifts are discussed in Scripture (Rom. 12:4-8; 1 Cor.12; Eph. 4:11-13). Spiritual gifts are supernatural motivations given to every believer. Paul relates spiritual gifts to the body. He mentions that there are varieties of "gifts, ministries and effect, but the same God" (1 Co.12:4-6). While there are many gifts, we normally look at only nine of them in our assessments. In the next chapter we will relate gifts, personality and leadership to church planting personnel.

Evangelism (Eph. 4:11)

People with the gift of evangelism have a desire to share Christ with the lost. They have an ability to communicate the gospel either individually or in a group context. It must be said that this gift is different from the mandate of God to all peoples to "make disciples of all the nations" (Matt. 28:19). Not every Christian has the gift of evangelism, but every Christian does have the mandate to share God's love with everyone they encounter.

Prophecy (Rom. 12:6)

Prophets today are not like the prophets we know in the Old Testament. However, like the prophets of old, today's prophets are bold in declaring the truth in spite of what others may think of them.

Teaching (Rom. 12:7; 1 Co. 12:28; Eph. 4:11)

Teachers have the ability to understand and communicate Scripture clearly and effectively. They like to study the Word and to help others get spiritual insight from the Bible.

Exhortation (Rom. 12:8)

Exhorters like to tell people what they need to do with truth. They feel a strong compassion toward those who are hurting. People with this gift are usually friendly, understanding and practical. They like to give advice and often are sought after for counsel.

Pastor/Shepherd (Eph. 4:11)

Pastors are encouragers. They have a strong motivation to lead and nurture the people of God. They give emphasis to harmony and are concerned about the spiritual health of God's flock.

Showing mercy (Rom. 12:8)

Those with the gift of mercy are sympathetic people. They have a passion to help those in difficult and crisis situations and provide support to help them through the crisis.

Ministry/Serving (Rom. 12:7)

This person serves joyfully behind the scenes. He or she usually is very flexible and adaptable. A servant often is energized by doing what no one else likes to do. The servant likes to be involved.

Giving (Rom. 12:8)

People with the gift of giving enjoy giving enthusiastically and prudently to others. Givers have unique financial insights. They would serve well on teams responsible for the finances in the church.

Administration (1 Co. 12:28)

Administrators like to deal with details, create a structure and staff those structures. They see the big picture and like to keep everyone moving toward the goal.

PERSONALITY

Everyone has a predictable pattern of behavior. There are four basic personality types. Normally, an individual will display a combination of style of temperament with one more dominant than the others. The work by Hippocrates in the first century and popularized by Tim LaHaye uses the terms choleric, sanguine, phlegmatic and melancholy. Another temperament tool is the Myers-Briggs Type Indicator (MBTI). It helps us understand how we handle practical areas of our lives. The (MBTI) helps (a) determine our preference for extroversion or introversion; (b) discover how we recognize information by preferring sensing or intuition; (c) discover how we make decisions through thinking or sensing; and (d) understand how we deal with the outer world involving our preference of judging or perceiving.[82]

A useful profile we use in the assessment of church planters is the DiSC, based on work by William Marston. DiSC is an acronym for the four behavioral temperament: Dominant, Influencing, Steadiness and Compliance.

Doers

These are extroverted and task-oriented people. They love challenges and are not afraid to take risks. They are decisive, determined and dominant. They need to guard not to hurt people in pursuit of the goal. The apostle Paul is a biblical example of a "doer."

Influencers

Also an extrovert who gets energized by being around people. These are people who like to have lots of fun and need approval and recognition from others. Like the doers, they too, will challenge the status quo. They need to learn to be more responsible than popular. Peter is a biblical example of an influencer.

Servants

This personality type is introverted and more people-oriented. They are submissive, steady, stable, security-oriented. S's types do not adapt to changes well, preferring more stability. They need to know that taking risks is sometimes necessary. Moses is a biblical example of a Servant.

Competent

An introvert and task-oriented person. This person is compliant, cautious and calculating. Motivated by quality and correctness they become perfectionist. Thomas is a biblical example of someone with a "C" personality.

While this chapter attempted to answer the question "Am I a Church Planter?" it is a worthwhile exercise for a new work team, nominating team, or the leadership of a local church to take the spiritual and personality profile. It will absolutely transform the way one looks at ministry.

CHARACTERISTICS OF A CHURCH PLANTER[83]

The last element of our comprehensive assessments for church planters is the behavioral interview. During the interview process, we require that both the church planter and the spouse be present for the interview, without exception. The rationale is that they are mobilized as a team and therefore need to participate together in this very important and determining part of the process. The interview seeks to isolate specific behaviors in the past that will predict future behavior. In this four-hour assessment, we explore thirteen different characteristics a church planter needs to exhibit. These characteristics were first identified by Charles Ridley and later slightly adapted by the Home Mission Board.[84] These are the thirteen behavioral characteristics as stated in the Basic Training Presenter's Manual (2001).

1. Visioning capacity – developing a theme that highlights the vision and philosophy of ministry and persuasively selling the vision to the people.

2. Intrinsically motivated – having initiative and aggressiveness without the negative connotations, having a willingness to work long and hard. Being a self-starter with a willingness to build from nothing.

3. Create ownership of ministry – helping people "buy in" and feel responsible for growth and success of the church, gaining commitment of the people to the vision.

4. Relates to lost – quickly getting to know the lost on a personal level, breaking through the barriers erected by the lost

5. Spousal support – having an explicit agreement regarding each partner's respective role and involvement in ministry.

6. Effectively build relationships – getting to know people on a personal basis, making others feel secure and comfortable in one's presence, appreciating and accepting a variety of style.

7. Committed to church growth – committing to numerical growth within the context of spiritual and relational growth.

8. Responsive to community – acquiring an understanding of the character and 'pulse" of the community.

9. Utilized giftedness of others – realizing and equipping people to do the task of ministry, discerning of spiritual gifts in others, matching the gifts of people with ministry needs and opportunities.

10. Flexible and adaptable – coping effectively with ambiguity and constant and abrupt change.

11. Builds group cohesiveness – incorporates newcomers into a network of relationships, dealing with conflict assertively, constructively and tactfully.

12. Resilience – experiencing setbacks without defeat, expecting the unexpected.

13. Exercises faith – believing in God's action, having a willingness to wait for answers to specific prayer requests.

ASSESSMENT FOLLOW-UP

A detailed written report is shared with the candidates. This is a growth time in which the assessor shares strengths, weaknesses and limitations based on the results of the assessment. Sometimes, assessments will confirm that there is much strength that points the couple toward a pastoral ministry rather than church planting. This is by no means failure on anyone's part. On the contrary, it illustrates the usefulness of the comprehensive assessment process. When this happens, a couple is rescued from possible frustration and eventually leaving the ministry.

Other times, the assessment process confirms that indeed there is a definite indication that the church planting team has a strong possibility of success. In times like this, we continue to work with the planter and the partner churches in preparation for that new church. One of the areas of preparation with both the planter and the partner deals with the personnel for church planting. This will be the topic of our next chapter.

REFLECTION
1. Read Ephesians 3:8 and 1 Timothy 2:7. Paul had a specific call to preach the gospel to a specific group. Can you think of God's specific call in your life? Describe how you are fulfilling God's call to you.

2. What are several values mentioned in this chapter about personal assessment and the interview assessment? How could you benefit from the personal assessment in your life?

3. Rick Warren's writings have popularized the concept of S.H.A.P.E.. This is an acronym for:
   Spiritual Gifts
   Heart or Passion
   Abilities
   Personality Type
   Experiences

What is your **passion** for ministry? Explain. How has God worked in your life to develop this passion?

4. Take the Spiritual Gifts and Personality (Temperament) inventories. What are your top three gifts? What is your dominant and secondary personality type?

5. What are the three lowest gifts? What can you do to strengthen them? What are things you must guard against in your personality? What practical steps will you take?

6. What, in your opinion, are the two top characteristics of the thirteen mentioned in this chapter? Why?

Personnel for Church Planting

While they were ministering to the Lord and fasting, the Holy Spirit said, "Set apart for me Barnabas and Saul for the work to which I have called them." Then, when they had fasted and prayed and laid their hands on them, they sent them away. . . When they reached Salamis, they began to proclaim the word of God in the synagogues of the Jews; and they also had John as their helper (Acts 13:2-3, 5).

There is a place for every believer to serve the Lord. The Bible speaks about the need for the body of Christ, the church, to work together for the expansion of the Kingdom of God. Paul, speaking of the many gifts in the body of Christ, reminded us of its purpose, ". . .for the equipping of the saints for the work of service, to the building up of the body of Christ. . ." (Eph. 4:12). We were created to fellowship with the Father and as a result of a healthy vertical relationship, we should enjoy fellowship with one another on earth. Aubrey Malphurs points out that Christ ministered through a team. He chose twelve men to spend three years with Him, He trained them and sent them out in teams (Mark 6:7). Paul also ministered through a team. That team consisted of Barnabas (Acts 11:22-30), Mark (Acts 13:2-3, 5), Silas (Acts 15:40), Timothy (Acts 16:1-3), Luke (Acts 16) and others.[85]

In the previous chapter we discussed the process for discovering if you are called to be a church planter. This chapter takes the called church planter and looks at how he/she selects team members for the new church plant.

SELECTING CHURCH PLANTER BY FUNCTION

The selection of a church planting team will be determined by the role the church planter plays. While others have given different names for the role of church planters, I will identify five positions we often see in our ministry.

Pastor/Church planter

This is the person who has a vision to start the church, develop it and remain as the pastor of that congregation. The people who will come to be part of the team must share the vision and values of the pastor. The individual gifts and personalities of team members should complement those of the pastor. He/she should be the key person in casting the vision before the people.

Church planter starter

This is the person God called to start new churches. However, his gifts are to start the church, develop initial leadership and then move on to start a new church in another area. These are people who start the congregation but leave the development to another. Usually, the church planter has strong gifts in evangelism, preaching and vision casting. He/she normally would be extroverted and people-oriented more than task-oriented.

Church planter catalyst

This would be the trainer/strategist with strong gifts in teaching, administration, vision casting and leadership. This person seeks to discover those whom God has called to church planting, provides on the job training (OJT), extension training, encourages and provides supervised opportunities for them.

People group church planter

This is the church planter called to serve among a specific people group, such as a language or a cultural group. If the planter is not of that specific group, there is a need for a cross-cultural ministry requiring understanding and knowledge of the people group. Normally people in this role have vision and do not fear stepping out on faith. They are good relational people.

Rescuers

Rescuers are church planters called specifically to serve in congregations that are declining and in need of "emergency surgical intervention." These planters are good at taking a dwindling congregation and creating an environment for growth. They are risk takers who are not easily discouraged.

DETERMINING ROLES OF CHURCH PLANTING TEAM MEMBER

The number of team members needed in a church planting team is determined by the gifts and personality of the planter. It is also determined by the specific needs of the target group to be reached. If a target group is young families, the priority is a quality nursery with trained workers. Other churches are more traditional and their priorities would include trained Sunday school workers.

CHURCH PLANTING AND PERSONALITY TYPES

The importance of the assessment is highlighted when you look at the relationships of assessment and performance in the field. Malphurs tells of a study of the personality profile of sixty-six church planters by the Christian Churches/Churches of Christ to correlate the personality type with the growth of their churches. The study revealed very interesting information. High D planters *Doers* had an average attendance of 72 after the first year and 181 after an average of 5.2 years. The high I's had an average of 98 after the first year and average of 174 after 3.6 *Influencers* years. The high S's had an average of 38 after the first year and 77 after 6.3 years. The high C's had an average of 39 *Compe...* after one year and 71 after 4.3 years.[86] Our tracking of church planters reveals the same patterns as the study by the Church of Christ. However, one interesting example that illustrates the importance of assessments and the follow-up is Ruben Ortega. Ruben is Pastor/ Church Planter of Sierra Vista Community Church in Las Cruces, New Mexico. This is an Hispanic culture/English speaking congregation. Ruben's personality type is S. After the first *Servant...* year, the average attendance was 37, which is in line with the study by the Church of Christ. After the third year, the average attendance of the church had tripled to 100. After the sixth year, the average attendance of the congregation is at 280. What made the difference? Ruben explained, that during the assessment follow-up visit, he was told that his personality would not allow him to lead the church to three hundred. "Knowing my weaknesses made me surround myself with a team that would complement those weaknesses." While it is important to use all tools available to us in church planting, it is wise for us to understand that God wants to do those things that are supernatural in our lives. "I can do all things through Him who strengthens me" (Phil. 4:13).

LEADERSHIP STYLE AND PERSONALITY TYPES

When discussing leadership, the question that usually comes to mind is, "Which style is best?" How would you answer that question? We will discuss briefly the relationship of personality to leadership styles.

Autocratic style

This style is characteristic of the high D leader. These are people who can make quick decisions and therefore are take-charge individuals. They love challenges and risks. They are good at solving problems and managing difficult situations.

Democratic style

This style is characteristic of the high I leader. These are the influencers and salespeople in the church. They are very impressive and articulate. They are excellent people to present the budget to your church as opposed to the D's who will probably bore the people with details. They prefer to work in teams and have the authority of making the final decision. Many worship leaders are I's.

Participatory style

This style is characteristic of the high S leader. They are very caring and loyal people. Changes could possibly make this type person very uncomfortable. They will make an effort for peace and tranquility. Confrontation is not part of their leadership style.

Bureaucratic style

This style is characteristic of the high C leader. This is the "perfectionist" leader, who loves detail and is competent and cautious. He likes to comply with policies and regulations.

Various situations call for different styles of leadership. An ideal leader would be one who is flexible enough to combine a task orientation with a people orientation. Some leaders recognize that they are not flexible enough to adapt their leadership styles to meet the needs of different situations, but are willing to complement those weaknesses with people whose strengths are in those areas.

REFLECTION

1. What are the five types of Church Planters listed in this chapter? Describe the functions of each. Can you identify some of these type planters in your area?

2. As you work with your "new work" team, which type of church planter do you need? Why?

3. What other members, in time, will the church planter need, in his team? These are some suggestions: Administrator, Teacher, Youth Worker, Worship Leader, evangelist, Children's Ministry, Cell Group Organizer and Church Planting Specialist. Which will he need as he starts? Why?

4. What personality type is your Church Planter? What are some strengths and weaknesses of that personality? What can he do to overcome the weaknesses? Be specific.

5. What is the leadership style of the Church Planter? Name the strengths and weaknesses.

CHAPTER *9*

The Role of the Laity in Church Planting

Now dispatch some men to Joppa and send for a man named Simon, who is also called Peter; he is staying with a tanner named Simon, whose house is by the sea (Acts 10:5-6).

Scripture shows that the movement of God, as seen in the church of the first century, was a lay-led movement. It makes sense to say that an organization is as good as its people. Unfortunately, churches today have great numbers of "unemployed" Christians. This chapter unveils God's plan for the laity, reasons for their uninvolvement, how to find meaning in ministry and some practical steps in mobilizing the laity. The abyss between the pulpit and the pew continues to widen. For the church to have a positive impact in its Jerusalem, Judea, Samaria and to the remotest part of the earth, this gulf must dry up and the people of God must get involved.

GOD'S PLAN

As mentioned in chapter four, no one is an island unto himself. The fact that Jesus Christ died at the cross to reconcile sinners to Himself and to bring together a group of believers is based on relationships. God's divine plan to unleash His people for service is seen: First, He wants to work through people. Scripture illustrates this fact in the life of Noah (Gen. 6:14); Nehemiah (Neh. 4:19-20); the

Samaritan Woman (John 4:39); Cornelius (Acts: 10:24); Paul and Barnabas (Acts 13:2-3); Peter (Acts 2:14); Philip (Acts 8:34-35). Second, He empowers us through the Holy Spirit. Therefore, it is not you, but God working through you. Luke 19:1-10 gives emphasis to the fact that Christ does all the work. He is the central piece of evangelism, He prepares a place for evangelism, "that place" (Luke 19:5), He seeks the person to evangelize "looked up"(Luke 19:5), Jesus calls people to repentance "Zaccheus, hurry and come down (Luke 19:5). Christ alone is able to bring genuine repentance (Luke 19:6, 8-9). Third, God has gifted us as part of the body of Christ for special service in order to build up the body of Christ (Eph. 4:7-12). Fourth, Every Christian is a minister (1 Pt. 2:5-9). Fifth, God wants to bless your life as you serve Him actively through your local congregation.

There is plenty to do in the Kingdom of God. You have a very important role to play. God wants to bless your life and all He asks of you is your availability.

REASONS FOR LACK OF INVOLVEMENT

I have heard for many years about the 20/80 principle. In essence, this principle tells us that twenty percent of the people in the church do the work of the other eighty percent of the people. As you can well imagine, this small group of faithful servants are usually exhausted and many times burned-out. George Gallup reports that this principle is actually too optimistic. He says that in actuality only ten percent of the people in the church are doing the work of the other ninety percent. Of the ninety percent, fifty percent say they will not become involved for whatever reason. The other forty percent say they would love to become involved but they have not been asked or trained.[87] As I have observed churches over the years, I *undeployed*

noticed some probable causes for the "unemployment" situation in our churches.

One reason may be the lack of intentional recruitment of lay leaders for specific jobs. A second reason is that pastors and staff members often do not communicate their expectations clearly to the laity. A third reason is that many people in the church are not aware of all the possible ministries or even that they could lead a new ministry. Fourthly, many of the laity feel they are called to do something in which training will not be provided. A fifth reason may be that the leadership of the church expects people to respond to information. Church members are not challenged or given a reason to respond. A sixth reason is that often times the laity do not feel they have a blessing from the leadership to reach out in areas such as church planting. A seventh reason may be the lack of expectations pastors have for the lay people in their churches. An eighth reason may be the lack of vision from the senior staff of the church.

This lack of involvement on the part of believers is a venom that is spreading and gradually extinguishing the life of the church. God indeed wants to bless you by working through your life.

FINDING SIGNIFICANCE IN MINISTRY

People want to do things that will bring significance to their lives. Cornelius and Peter were like that, as are so many of us. Cornelius was a Roman soldier and a devout man who feared God (Acts 10: 2). Peter was a pompous Jewish man. It seemed these two did not have a lot in common. But they had at least three very important ingredients that brought significance to their lives. These ingredients are for our lives as well. One was that they were *ordinary people.* You may ask the question, who was

Moses? He was an ordinary man but, because of his commitment, God did extraordinary things through the ordinary man Moses. God used Moses to lead the Israelites out of captivity. Who was Joshua? He was an ordinary man but, because of his commitment, God did extraordinary things through the ordinary man Joshua. God used Joshua to lead His people to the promise land. Who was Paul? He was an ordinary man but, because of his commitment to Christ, he was used in an extraordinary manner. To date, Paul is the greatest church planter we have ever seen. What about you? I believe that the greatest chapter of your life is yet to be written. But, it will depend on your commitment to the Lordship of Jesus Christ.

A second ingredient is *prayer*. The Bible says that Cornelius prayed continually (Acts 10:2). You and I might design wonderful and impressive plans and strategies before man. But unless all our plans are immersed in prayer, everything will crumble as cookies in the hands of a child.

A third ingredient is *obedience*. Cornelius obeyed God by sending a delegation to Joppa (Acts 10: 5 –6). In Joppa, Peter, was being prepared by God to understand that "What God had cleansed, no longer consider unholy" (Acts 10:15). Neither of these men knew what was going to happen next but they were keeping their eyes and ears attentive to God, who knows all things. "Cornelius was waiting for them and had called together his relatives and close friends" (Acts 10:24). This lay person continued to work with people in his neighborhood in preparation for the coming of Peter. Peter, a Jew, preached the gospel of Jesus Christ to a room full of Italian people. It was a cross-cultural revival. It was successful because both of these men were obedient.

MOBILIZING THE LAITY

Many of the new congregations started after the Saddleback model are using some variation of the three stages described in this section. The discovery stage, the follow-up stage and the ministry stage provide congregations with a systematic process of evaluating, consulting and placing the people of God in ministries that will match their spiritual gifts.

The discovery stage provides an explanation of God's design for each of us. In this stage believers discover their passions, spiritual gifts, personalities and their leadership styles (explained in Chapters Seven and Eight).

The follow-up stage provides interpretation of the inventories previously taken and suggestions of possible personal ministries. In other words, it is a session to match person to ministry.

The ministry stage provides discovery of the ministry niche of the lay person. Those ministries can be inside or outside the church or both. Lay persons and ministry leaders are matched to form teams. The ministry leader will be responsible for the equipping of the lay person.

I trust that you will be on fire to serve the Lord Jesus. Remember, He desires to work through you, an ordinary person and accomplish extraordinary things through you. Go for it!

REFLECTION

1. What reasons are given for God's divine plan to unleash His people? Can you think of other reasons?

2. As you examined your church, would the 20/80 principle be applicable? Why or Why not? What additional reasons can you add for not getting involved?

3. What three ingredients for significance in ministry were discussed in this chapter? What is your opinion of the ingredients? Do you need to change anything in your life? How do you plan to do it? Be specific and write it down.

4. What three stages for mobilizing the laity were discussed in this chapter? Does your church have a similar process? If not, could this possibly make a difference?

10 Developing a Farm System

You did not choose Me but I chose you and appointed you that you would go and bear fruit and that your fruit would remain, so that whatever you ask of the Father in My name He may give to you (John 15: 6).

Those of us who enjoy the game of baseball cannot wait for that spring day when the umpire shouts "PLAY BALL!" Some players will be assigned to instructional leagues, others to rookie leagues; others will play minor league baseball in class A, AA, or AAA. Others will get the chance of a lifetime and play in the majors. As the season progresses you hear news of players being sent down to the minors and others being called up to the majors.

The farm system provides opportunities for players to be developed and groomed for the next level. Corporations are constantly training and promoting people for the next level. The army trains, develops and promotes soldiers to the next levels of responsibility.

Churches can also develop a farm system. I believe that people in churches are probably the most trained people on the face of the earth. But, the farm system goes beyond the training to the actual placing of people in ministries. This chapter will suggest some simple ways to develop the next generation of church planters. The farm system is about winning the lost through the multiplication of new converts, new leadership, new units and new congregations.

One of the responsibilities of the pastor is to lay a foundation upon which he can build an effective reproducible ministry for the future. This takes time and effort. I know firsthand because I am the product of this farm system in my home church in Maryland. My pastor and my Sunday school teacher took the time to provide training to a handful of people, but practical opportunities for ministries always were part of that training. The book that has most effectively transformed my life is *The Master Plan of Evangelism* by Robert E. Coleman. In this book, Coleman shares eight principles.[88] While evangelism is the emphasis, I believe these principles are applicable to the development of a "Farm System" for your church. Robert Coleman reminds us, "A few people so dedicated in time will shake the world for God. Victory is never won by the multitudes."[89] Take time to mentor a few people who, in time, will transform communities for Christ.

These are the eight keys to development of Church planters:[90]

SELECTION

Jesus worked through people who were willing to learn. He concentrated on a few and poured His life and entire ministry into those few. As you look at the people God has placed in your church, pray and ask the Lord to raise those whom He has called. What an awesome responsibility!

DEVELOP RELATIONSHIPS

Spend time developing strong relationships with those around you. In the farm system, knowledge is taught more by association than by a particular curriculum. This puts pressure on you, the leader, to be like Jesus. The apostle Paul said, "Therefore I exhort you, to be imitators of me" (1 Co. 4:16). Jesus's purpose in selecting the few was "that they would be with Him and that He could send them out to preach" (Mk. 3:14). Notice that the sending was after they had spent time with Him.

COMMITMENTS

One of the expectations of both the leader and his group should be a commitment to each other and to the farm system process. The fact that so many believers today are immature in their spiritual growth is an indication of a lack of commitment to Christ. Another part of the problem is that many leaders of the church settle for mediocrity. Many of them were never part of a "farm system." They never had a committed role-model to help them grow strong in Christ.

GIVE YOURSELF AWAY

Remember that before you can give yourself away, you must possess that which you are to give away. Christ gave away His love (Jn. 13:34); His joy (Jn. 15:11); His life (Jn. 3:16); and His peace (Jn. 14:27). He also gave the disciples His burning passion for a lost world. You can also make a difference in the life of people as you give yourself away.

SHOW THEM HOW TO DO IT

Jesus taught in a practical and informal classroom setting. His informality is hard to understand in a day in which we are so technologically advanced. He showed them how to pray (Mt. 6:9); He showed them the importance of Scripture (Mk. 12:10, Jn. 13:18-19); He showed them how to live in the world (Mt. 25:34, Jn. 16:33); He showed them how to deal with controversy and conflicts (Lk. 23:33); He showed them about mission (Lk. 9:12); His training was ongoing (Mk. 4); and He showed them about life (Mk. 9:35-37).

GIVE THEM A JOB TO DO

Provide on-the-job training (OJT) for those that are part of the farm system. There should be very practical opportunities for ministry. Jesus knew when His disciples were ready to put their training into practice. He took them along and gave them assignments (Mt. 9:35-38); He sent the twelve out (Lk. 9:1); He briefed them and reminded them to expect opposition to their ministry (Mt. 10:22); and He sent them out two by two. What jobs are your farm team able to do now? Give them something meaningful to do.

CHECK ON THEM

One of the strongest negative reactions I have received is from those who do not want personal accountability. After the disciples returned from their assignments, they "gathered together with Jesus; and they reported to Him all that they had done and taught" (Mk. 6:30). In the feeding of the five thousand, Jesus used that opportunity to check on their spiritual discernment. He shared four principles with them:

Principle of sharing

The disciples' solution was "send the crowds away" (Mt. 14:15). Jesus' solution was "You give them something to eat" (Mt. 14:16).

Principle of simplicity

"We have here only five loaves and two fish"(Mt. 14:17). The lesson here is that God can multiply a simple offering in tremendous ways. Can you imagine how much God could do with your life, if you will simply yield to Him?

Principle of strengthening

The Lord used this event to strengthen the faith of His disciples.

Principle of servanthood

"The disciples gave them to the crowds" (Mt. 14:19). He taught them a lesson about "going" and "serving" people. Three important stones on which we must intentionally step are: giving of ourselves, going to serve the people of God and growing as we journey together.

MULTIPLY

Jesus expected His disciples to multiply and bear fruit (Jn. 15:1-17). You are part of the body of Christ because someone took the time to tell you about Jesus. Will you be faithful in doing the same?

It is my hope that I have shared some thoughts in this chapter that will plant seeds in your life and that the seed would grow to the point of transforming your ministry.

REFLECTION

1. Explain what is meant by a farm system?

2. What are the eight keys to development of church planters? Can you help in the development of another person? Who? How will you approach this individual?

3. In the section "check on them" you will find four principles based on Matthew 14:14-19. What are they? Are these principles part of your life? If they are not, why not? List reasons.

— What adjustments do you need to make in your life in order to adopt these four principles?

Identifying the Called-out

Practical steps I can take

1. Develop a simple form that church members can fill out and return to the new work group. This form should ask for name, address, telephone and choices for interest in church planting such as: opened my home to a Bible study, visitation, survey, I like to explore lay church planting, prayer walking, telephone survey, etc.

2. Offer a "Discovering your passion" to members of your church.*

3. Offer a "Discovering your Spiritual Gifts and Personality" inventory.*

4. Study the life of Nehemiah, Paul, Peter and Phillip. Give particular attention to how God works through people like you, the Holy Spirit's role in the life of these men and the way God gifted each men.

5. As a "new work" team take a survey in your congregation to discover why people are not involve in the ministries of the church.

6. Maybe you can begin to practice the eight principles mentioned in Chapter ten. You definitely can be use of God to have a positive impact in the life of those God will bring to you.

*You may obtain the passion and spiritual gifts and personality inventories by contacting Dr. Gustavo V. Suárez at: GSuarez403@aol.com

Equipping the Church Planter

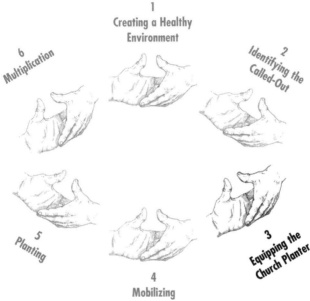

1
Creating a Healthy
Environment

6
Multiplication

2
Identifying the
Called-Out

5
Planting

3
Equipping the
Church Planter

4
Mobilizing

This section will provide a description of some basic tools needed for church planting. While there are many areas in which church planters should be equipped, I have chosen four that are critical. It is not the intent of these chapters to describe in detail how to equip a church planter or even exhaust the topic. The pages that follow will provide principles, ideas and suggestions that can strengthen your ministry. Equipping is not a one-time event; it is ongoing throughout the entire church planting process. The chapters in this section discuss evangelism, development of relationships, small groups and the role of the partner church. A key word for the section is "nurture."

11 ## The Importance of Evangelism in Church Planting

The woman said to Him, "Sir, give me this water, so I will not be thirsty nor come all the way here to draw" (Jn. 4:15).

Today there are numerous warning signs about the future of evangelism. Southern Baptists, the largest protestant denomination, report that 19.1% of member churches did not baptize one person in 2001. Another way to look at this sad statistic is that nearly one in five churches in the Southern Baptist Convention did not baptize one person in 2001.[91] Chart 5 (on the next page) illustrates a steady increase in the number of churches reporting from 0 to 5 baptisms between 1996 and 2001.

Chart 5

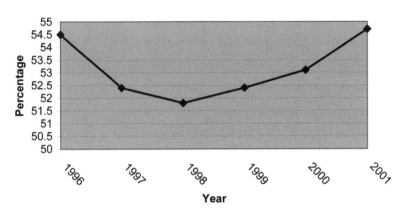

Source: Annual Church Profile, LifeWay Christian Resource Center, Nashville, Tenn.; compiled by Dr. Gustavo V. Suárez, Baptist Convention of New Mexico, Albuquerque, NM.

	Churches Baptizing Five or Less 1996-2001	
DATE	PERCENTAGE	NUMBER OF CHURCHES
1996	54.5	20,369
1997	52.4	19,702
1998	51.8	19,081
1999	52.4	19,661
2000	53.1	19,693
2001	54.7	20,474

Chart 6 (on the next page) reveals a persistent, steady increase in the number of churches that did not baptize anyone in a given year from 1972 to 2001. The most significant improvement in the thirty years happened between 1979 and 1980 with a decrease of nearly two percent. Many pastors and church leaders never have led a person to Christ.

Chart 6

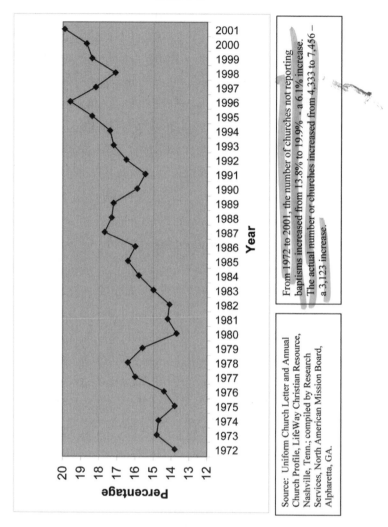

From 1972 to 2001, the number of churches not reporting baptisms increased from 13.8% to 19.9% – a 6.1% increase. The actual number of churches increased from 4,333 to 7,456 – a 3,123 increase.

Source: Uniform Church Letter and Annual Church Profile, LifeWay Christian Resource, Nashville, Tenn.; compiled by Research Services, North American Mission Board, Alpharetta, GA.

It is reasonable to conclude that if the leadership of the church is not intentional about evangelism, the people in the church will not be intentional in their evangelistic outreach. Add to this the disintegration of the family and the picture gets gloomier. One cannot grow a healthy, reproducible congregation without an intentional plan for evangelism.

George Barna reports that despite their evangelistic reputation, only four out of ten adults attending Baptist churches shared their faith with a non-believer in the past year. Evangelism is not an option for the church planter.

THE CURRENT CONDITION OF EVANGELISM

1. Believers are isolated from the lost – They may work next to an unbeliever but the reality is that many Christians do not have many lost people in their circle of friends.

2. Irrelevant methodology will not reach the lost – The approaches of the past will not work today. The boomers, busters and bridgers ranging in age between 27 and 58 make up 72% of the U.S. population. Their way of thinking is very different and requires new methodologies to reach them.

3. Churches have lost sight of the unchurched population – The United States has shifted from a churched to an unchurched culture. Yet, we continue to try to reach the lost with the same approaches used in 1950 and 1960.

CULTURALLY RELEVANT EVANGELISM

Many ministries of the church do not match the needs of the people outside the church. This is not the only reason, but certainly an important reason for the increasing numbers of plateaued and declining churches. The following are some suggestions you may use to develop a plan for evangelism.

1. *Who is your neighbor?*
   a. Discover the unchurched and unsaved people in your community.
   b. Get to know the unchurched and unsaved people.
   c. Ask questions to determine why they are not attending church or have not accepted Christ.
   d. What are churches in your community doing to reach these groups of people?

2. *How can we create a positive image in the community?*
   a. Show a genuine desire to reach the lost in that community.
   b. The church planter and his team must build relationships with people in the community.
   c. As the church planting team gets to know the people and the needs of the community, they can minister to the real, felt and anticipated needs of the unchurched of the community.
   d. Use multimedia marketing, direct mail and newspapers. Consider the target group you are trying to reach and how they would react to your strategies. Use media wisely.
   e. Identify and penetrate key people networks. John the Baptist demonstrated the importance of penetrating people networks. Andrew heard John the Baptist speak about Jesus and followed in search of the Lord. He then found his brother Simon Peter. The next day Jesus found Philip who then brought Nathanael to Jesus (John 1:40-47).
   f. Intentionally share the gospel with non-believers. Make it a practice to share the gospel with the lost.
   g. Equip others for evangelism. Think reproduction!

3. *What are your ministry opportunities?*
   Now that you have some idea of the community and the needs of the people list some simple and realistic ministries to reach the community.

A BIBLICAL EXAMPLE

Jesus was sitting by Jacob's well when a Samaritan woman came to draw water. Jesus said, "Give me a drink"(John 4:7). The dialogue ended with her request, "Sir, give me this water, so I will not be thirsty nor come all the way here to draw"(John 4:15). This is the best example anywhere in Scripture of sharing the gospel with a lost person. Notice the two dialogues. Jesus stayed with the topic of water, each time revealing additional information. The Samaritan woman, on the other hand, was thinking religion and how it related to her culture. Does that sound familiar? Look at some principles used by Jesus during this divine encounter.

1. He looked for that which was common, "water" (John 4:7).

2. He attempted to neutralize existing barriers (John 4:9).

3. He shared only necessary information (John 4:10).

4. He gave additional information about this water (John 4:13).

5. After she asked for the water of life, He expected her to repent. He did this by saying to her "Go call your husband and come here"(John 4:16-18).

6. He responded to her religious statements (John 4:21-24).

Evangelism is key to any church planting effort. It is foundational in the equipping of church planters. "Go therefore and make disciples. . ." (Mt. 28:19).

REFLECTION

1. How was the current condition of evangelism described in this chapter? Do you agree with the author? What else can you add?

2. Think of your present ministry. Follow the suggestions to develop a plan for evangelism. Who is your neighbor? How can we create a positive image? What ministry opportunities do we have? Helpful sources for demographical information are:

— Census Bureau www.census.gov
— Percept
— Local library
— Local or state denominational

3. Study John 4:7-45. What else can you learn about evangelism from these verses?

12 *Development of Relationships*

Abide in Me and I in you. As the branch cannot bear fruit of itself unless it abides in the vine, so neither can you unless you abide in Me. I am the vine, you are the branches; he who abides in Me and I in him, he bear much fruit, for apart from Me you can do nothing (John 15:4-5).

THE IMPORTANCE OF RELATIONSHIPS

*T*he development of healthy relationships is critical to the planting of healthy, reproducible churches. Relationships speak to the connection of persons within the church. The Bible is a book about relationships and ministry develops through relationships. Healthy relationships begin with a strong walk with the Lord.

RELATIONAL NETWORKS

The church planting family should reflect healthy relationships at home. Church planting is hard work and the last thing the planter needs is a non-supportive family. Spousal support is key in the assessment process (see chapter seven). The planting family can draw support from many sources. It is crucial for the planting family to develop this relational network of support if they are to survive a new church start.

The **mentor** *is a friend to the planter.*

This is a person who can guide, encourage, affirm and hold the planter accountable. He is not interested only in the new work, but in the person and family of the planter. In our ministry we have very effectively used a *technical mentor*. This is a practitioner who is able to guide the new planter in the more technical aspects of the church start in such things as getting a mail permit, incorporation, etc.

The **intercessory prayer team** *supports not only the plant, but the planter's family as well.*

In the reflection section, suggestions will be given on ways to develop this team.

The **church planting team** *is determined by the role the church planter plays (chapter eight).*

Building healthy relationships with the team will produce a healthy church start. This team is instrumental in building a team around the vision, core values and mission statements of the church. In some cases, there may be very little difference between this team and the core group. I see this team giving guidance, after launching the church, to the initial work of the core group.

The **partnership group** *provides outside resources for the church.*

The lead partner may enlist other partner churches to help in the church plant. Partner churches can help by providing team members, core group members, finances, supplies, equipment and assistance in their planning. Another group related to the partner groups is the local community of churches. Two other groups in this partnership are the state and national agency for your denomination. They can add resources in terms of demographics, finances and expertise. A fifth partner is the church planter's network (CPN). This is a group of like-minded individuals meeting informally, but regularly, to learn from each other.

The core group *is the new church in seed form.*

This will be discussed more fully in chapter nineteen. These are the initial people committed to the vision, values and mission of the new work.

The ministry team *is developed as the church grows.*

As these new relationships evolve, new ministries or even new churches may be started. For example, as people interact in their relational networks, a new church may see a need to start a sports ministry or a different ministry. Whatever is done, the purpose should always be to reach people for Christ.

REACHING PEOPLE THROUGH RELATIONSHIPS

In January 1983, my wife and I moved to Buffalo, New York to start a new church. We walked up and down many streets, visiting door to door. One day we came to the door of Arcadio and Luz Martinez. We shared with them our intentions of starting a new congregation. Immediately they asked us to come in and treated us as old friends. They became the *person of peace.* Arcadio and Luz were gatekeepers to our entry into the Spanish neighborhood in Buffalo. Biblical examples of the person of peace are Andrew (Jn. 1:35-36), Matthew (Mt. 9:9-10), Cornelius (Acts 10), Lydia (Acts 16:13-15) and the jailer (Acts 16: 16-34). The next thing that developed out of our new and growing relationship was that the Martinezes introduced us to their children and their children's families who, in turn, knew other people interested in a new work in Buffalo *(the family of the person of peace)*. Arcadio and Luz introduced us to many of their friends in that neighborhood *(friends of the person of peace)*. As a result, new relationships with new friends meant more acquaintances and more prospects for the church. Soon the Iglesia Bautista Puente de Paz was started with these people as the core. Healthy relationships are important for the start of healthy congregations.

REFLECTION

1. Examine your relationship with the Lord. Spend time alone in prayer and ask God to show you areas in your life that need changing. List those areas. How do you plan to address each of the items in your list. Do you see how an unhealthy relationship with the Lord affects other relationships?

2. What is the role of the mentor? Do you have a mentor? In what ways has the mentor helped you personally and in your ministry? Do you have a written covenant?

3. Do you have an intercessory prayer team? If not, these are suggestions that may help you in starting one.
   — Look for people with a passion for the lost and for church planting
   — Look for people that are already people of prayer
   — Look for people that have demonstrated interest in you, your family and   ministry.

4. Write a letter to the people you want to ask to be part of your intercessory team.
   — Develop an invitational piece
   — Include a covenant agreement that reflects respon-sibilities on both sides
   — Develop an ongoing communication plan for requesting prayer and updating the team

5. Can you identify the person of peace in your ministry? Who is that person? How was this person instrumen-tal in opening opportunities for ministries?

13 Small Groups

Day by day continuing with one mind in the temple, and break-
ing bread from house to house, they were taking their meals
together with gladness and sincerity of heart (Acts 2:46).

PURPOSE OF SMALL GROUPS

This chapter is a natural extension of the previous chapter on relationships. Recently I was reviewing a study of a congregation that was intentionally evangelistic. However, they scored very low in the area of relationships and consequently, also scored very low in the area of small groups. There is a definite connection between relationships and small groups. The principal purpose of small groups is to support spiritual growth. Small groups also facilitate the development of new relationships, minimizing the number of people going out the back door. Small groups sometimes become new congregations. Malphurs states that "75 to 90 percent come to faith in Christ through a significant relationship with another person."[92] The reality is that many more people come to know Jesus through significant relationships with others than through a message.

THE BIBLE TEACHES ABOUT SMALL GROUPS

The Book of Acts records the phenomenal growth of the early church. They needed some type of organization to minister to the large numbers of people. Rick Warren advocates that "we must grow larger and smaller at the same time." The church in Jerusalem began in the upper room with 120 persons (Acts 1:15). About 3,000 people responded to Peter's sermon and were baptized into the church (Acts 2:41). The Lord "was adding to their number day by day those who were being saved" (Acts 2:47). Peter and John were speaking to the people and "those who heard the message believed; and the number of the men came to be about five thousand" (Acts 4:4). The persecution of the church served to spread the gospel and start new churches.

There were large meetings primarily used for evangelism (Acts 4:4; 5:42); preaching (Acts 20:20); and teaching (Acts 5:42).[93] Small groups intended to provide community. The three primary functions were ministry (Acts 4:32-37); worship and breaking bread (Acts 2:46); and teaching and preaching (Acts 5:42).

FUNCTIONS OF SMALL GROUPS.

There are several ways to organize small groups. These may include geography, dependence problems, common interests, home groups, discovery groups, Sunday school groups and ministry tasks. Healthy small groups will normally include four functions. (a) discover – time to explore new principles, (b) love – the extension of God's love through you to others in the group, (c) act – any healthy group must include a "doing" part and (d) make a decision – this is an important part of any small group.

CHARACTERISTICS OF SMALL GROUPS

Small groups help facilitate the building of relationships. A typical group should have nine to fifteen members. This allows for people to know each other and to share life's pilgrimage. (b) Small groups are repro-ducible. Because groups lose their effectiveness beyond fifteen, it is imperative that they reproduce and form a new group. (c) Small groups help in the development of new leadership. Every group needs to have an assistant-in-training that is being developed to be the leader of a future small group. (d) Small groups are often very effec-tive in attracting new groups of people. Small groups grow faster than large groups. (e) Small groups decen-tralize pastoral care. As churches grow, more of the pastoral responsibilities must be placed in the hands of small group members. (f) Small groups are not limited by finances. These groups are normally lay-led and the cost, if any, is very minimal. (g) Small groups are not limited by facilities. They can meet at someone's office, home, in a park and at different times.

Churches are made up of people. People need mean-ingful relationships. While there are people who can relate in large groups, many feel more comfortable with only a few people. Small groups provide the latter with that opportunity. In the past, churches grew out of small group Bible studies. Today, most church planters nurture people through Bible study, out of which a core group develops. Leaders are trained, while values, vision and mission statements are discovered and then the new church is launched. These approaches are different from those of the past, but small groups continue to play a key part in starting new churches.

REFLECTION

1. If you have started a small group, list your group by type and evaluate its effectiveness in relationship to its purpose.

2. Suggest how an effective small group structure can result in the starting of a multiplying church movement.

3. Do you agree with the statement that "many people come to Christ through a significant relationship with another person?" How did you come to Christ?

4. What was the intention of small groups in the early church? What were the three primary functions of small groups mentioned in Acts 2:46; 4:32-37; and 5:42?

5. Mention different types of small groups? What four functions are normally part of a healthy small group?

6. If you are part of a small group, review the characteristics of the small groups. Do you see those characteristics in your group?

7. If you do not belong to a small group, what advantages and disadvantages do you see? In terms of spiritual and physical advantages? What about your involvement? Are you more likely to be involved in a small group or a large group of people (church)?

14 The Role of the Lead Partner

When they arrived at Jerusalem, they were received by the church and the apostles and the elders and they reported all that God had done with them (Acts 15:4).

The lead partner was excited about starting a new congregation. The pastor worked with a group from his church in the preparation for the birth of a new congregation. The prospective pastor for the new work visited the area and was interviewed by the leadership group from the lead church. The pastor of the lead church attended basic and mentor training for church planters. While he was there, I began to observe the emergence of some red flags. Statements such as, "I have all the plans" and, "I'll just tell him what to do and he will do it," led me to believe there were problems on the horizon. A few months later, emergency intervention was required. Unfortunately, this story is not an isolated incident in relationships between the lead partner and the new work. This chapter will offer suggestions for the responsibilities of the lead partner and the new congregation.

INITIAL PREPARATIONS

The following suggestions assume that the pastor is guided by a clear vision from God to start a new congregation. The initial preparations for a new church begin within the walls of the lead church. Remember, the more people that are involved in this venture, the greater the chances of ownership by the lead church. Therefore, *cultivation* of the people within the lead church becomes critical to the success of the new work. Cultivation starts with the selection of a "new work" team. The responsibility of this team is to communicate positively and regularly with the church body as to the progress of the new work and the need for both human and financial resources. This team also will be the liaison between the partner church and the new congregation. The purpose of cultivation is to discover potential members, create an interest in the community about the new church to be started and to determine needs of the community.

The *"new work"* team can prepare the lead church for the exciting journey ahead. This can be done in very creative ways. During a worship service, a short play highlighting the fun of church planting, short testimonies or announcements in the new work corner could be given. A five-minute presentation by a local representative from the city planning commission might be helpful in understanding projected growth. Again, this sort of preparation must be ongoing. Think of it as the excitement and preparation of a couple ready to have a baby. They just cannot stop talking about the plans for the future of this baby.

The lead partner, through the studies of demographics and psychographics, *selects a place* where a new church is needed. The demographic data provides helpful information such as a comparison between the number of persons currently living in an area and the population ten years earlier. This type of data shows whether an area is growing or declining. Demographic data also reveals the ages and cultural backgrounds of the residents of a specific community or neighborhood. This is important in determining your target group, type of worship and type of church plant. The type of housing and the socio-economic level will help determine the needs of the community. The type of employment and family structure will be additional information that will help the church planter determine the ministries to pursue. If the community has a high number of young married couples, it may indicate that ministries to young families is something the new church could offer. A psychographic study can give the planter a profile of the lifestyles and socio-economic levels of the residents of that community. At this point, some people from the lead church may start cultivating Bible studies in different homes in the selected area. Additional events helpful at this point are: prayer walking, surveying the area and block parties.

CHURCH PLANTING PARENTING MODELS

Some people are adamant that only "churches start churches." While that may fit the ecclesiology of some denominations, the reality remains that only God starts churches. He may choose a person or a group of individuals or churches to start a new church. There is certainly value in churches starting churches but that is not the only method. These are some parenting models for your consideration.

Lead partner – new church

Colonizing – the lead partner sends a group of people to form the core group for the new church. There are several advantages to this method. First, the new church has a group of leaders from the start. Second, there is a financial base from those new members. Third, there is a link to the lead partner and its customs. Fourth, there is a doctrinal understanding from the beginning. However, one must also look at the possible disadvantages of this model. First, the core group may want to start the same type of church as the lead partner church. Second, they may not be interested in reaching new people from the community. Third, they may feel comfortable with maintaining the status quo. Fourth, they might resist changes the new pastor initiates. Fifth, they may develop an attitude of owning the church that results in the exclusion of newcomers.

Members on loan – similar to the colonizing method, except that the core group does not plan to stay as part of the new church. Their role is to provide the new work with initial leadership, finances and doctrinal stability. The return of the core group to the lead partner should be arranged in such a way that not everyone leaves at the same time. This could be very detrimental to the development of the new church. In some cases, people may feel led to remain with the new congregation rather than return to the sponsoring or lead church.

Lead partner – satellite congregation

This method of parenting has the potential to enlarge the Kingdom by starting satellite congregations in different areas of the city and touching people from different language and cultural backgrounds. One advantage of this model is that the satellite congregations can benefit from the fact that the established congregation is known in that community. Another benefit is that many satellite congregations can meet in apartments and other small, inexpensive places, thereby reducing the financial burden on both the lead and satellite congregations.

Lead partner – revitalization plan

A church should take seriously the responsibility of partnering with a plateaued or declining congregation in order to provide revitalization and refocus. An agreement detailing the expectations of both congregations is a wise beginning. Normally, in this type of model, the lead partner has a transitioning committee made up of representatives of both congregations. "Change" is an essential ingredient for this model. Many of the suggestions and ideas presented above under initial preparation would be applicable at this time.

Lead partner – reclamation plan

This model is a variation of the revitalization plan. The church is disbanded and all assets turned over to the lead partner. After examining the factors that contributed to the disbanding of the congregation, the lead partner initiates a study of the community. A determination is made of the type of church and planter needed in that community. Again, the suggestions and ideas mentioned under initial preparation are applicable at this stage. Some advantages are: a facility is already in place, the lead partner has access to new leadership and both human and financial resources available to help the new work. One disadvantage may be that the church's attitude and reputation could be hard to overcome in the community, thus requiring community outreaches to repair the image of the church. Another disadvantage may be the high cost of upkeep and repairs of the existing building.

CHURCH PLANTING PARTNERING MODEL[94]

Multiple sponsorship

This model is seen more often today than in previous years. It is used in areas where the established churches are not strong enough financially, yet there is a need for a new work. I always recommend guidelines in order to clarify expectations, but this is especially important in multiple sponsorships. A lead partner is selected to work along side other partners. This will minimize, if not prevent, any disagreement in the roles of all the partner churches. All financial arrangements should go through the lead partner.

Multi-congregational

This model is particularly suited for multicultural cities. Many congregations are not able to afford property of their own. However, by sharing a building and pooling resources, congregations can accomplish many positive things. An excellent example of this model is 19th Avenue Baptist Church in San Francisco, California. There are five congregations (Anglo, Chinese, Arabic, Vietnamese and Japanese) meeting in one building. While there are many advantages to this model, one needs to be certain that very clear lines of communication and covenants are in place before pursuing this approach.

Church planting training center

Otto Arango, a Hispanic minister in McAllen, Texas, established a church planting center. In two years, the center trained fifty lay people and bivocational ministers who started twenty churches. Arango caught a vision for starting other centers around the state. In 1999, the students in these centers started 105 churches as a result of his ministry. Can you see the potential for new churches that could be started through church planting centers?

RELATIONAL STYLES OF LEAD PARTNERS[95]

Relationships between partner churches and new work are important. Unfortunately, some partner churches are partner churches in name only. This discourages the people involved in the church planting partnerships. They are attempting to operate with different expectations. The following are some relational styles of partnering churches.

Retired grandparent

These are churches that would love to participate in the sponsoring of a new work; however, they really do not have the energy or the time to take full responsibilities in raising a new baby. Like grandfathers, they really enjoy the grandkids but do not want to raise them.

Protective parent

These churches are reluctant to give responsibilities to the new work for fear that they are not yet capable of doing things on their own. As the new work grows they want, like children, to take on more responsibilities and do things differently but find that they do not have a lot of freedom.

Demanding parent

These churches are very demanding of their new work. They expect the baby to act like an adult and at times it seems as if nothing they do is right.

"Depression Era" parent

These are the churches that are financially secure and have leaders who could be assets to the new work. Yet, their philosophy is "I struggled, so therefore you can learn as you struggle."

Adult parent

These churches are those that know when to be strict and when to be lenient. They know when to play with you and when to be serious. But at all times they know how to love and care for the new work.

RESPONSIBILITIES OF BOTH LEAD PARTNER AND NEW CONGREGATION [96]

The following are only some of the recommended responsibilities of the sponsor churches, other partners and the new congregations.

Sponsor church and partners

1. Assume spiritual, financial and legal responsibility for the church.

2. Work with the core group of the new church in planning cultivating events.

3. Publicize the new church start.

4. Start home Bible studies.

5. Plan for joint Sunday services with the emerging new church.

6. Secure a meeting facility and pay for the rent for an agreed period of time.

7. Identify and hire first pastor.

8. Assist with the pastors's salary, travel, housing and insurance for an agreed period of time. Work with the leadership of the new church.

9. Provide joint training and fellowship events for the new congregation.

10. Work together with the pastor and leader of the new congregation in plans for constituting the church.

11. Provide weekly prayer support.

12. Supply Bibles, literature and hymnals.

13. Enlist and mobilize youth and adults to do surveys, Backyard Bible Clubs, Vacation Bible Schools, evangelism training and visitation.

14. Help with the moving expenses of the new pastor.

New congregation

1. The new congregation chooses to teach, preach and practice sound biblical doctrine.

2. The new congregation will be loyal to their denomination. They will also establish healthy relationships between all partners.

3. The new congregation will regularly contribute to missions causes.

4. The new congregation will plan its own program and adopt a budget in partnership with the partner churches.

5. The new congregation will establish financial maturity and move toward self-support.

6. The new congregation will identify, train and mobilize potential leaders.

7. The new congregation will organize its programs and ministries.

8. The new congregation will organize ministries to reach surrounding communities.

9. The new congregation will teach the people to be a multiplying congregation.

Many congregations do not have sufficient resources to do everything on the list. It is for this reason that partnering with other churches becomes essential for the success and satisfaction of all partners.

REFLECTION
1. What are some things your church can do to cultivate the people for a healthy church plant?

2. Look at the census information for your area. (www.census.gov). What was the population ten years ago? What is the population today? Is the population growing or declining? What are factors contributing to the growth or decline?

3. Look at the population in terms of Anglos, Hispanics, African American and other ethnic groups? What is the percentage of the population? Are there churches ministering to that specific group? List these churches. If there are no churches for that specific target group, what can be done about it?

4. Study the church planting parenting models mentioned in the chapter. Have you had experience with any of these? Share your experience both positive and negative. What could have been done differently?

5. Study the church planting partnering models mentioned in the chapter. Which of these models would be appropriate for your area? Explain. What are some advantages and disadvantages of each?

6. What relational styles have you experienced in church planting? Why do you think that particular relational style was used? Was it effective or not? How would you have changed the approach?

7. Look over the responsibilities for both the lead partner and the new church. From that list, what are some things you can do personally? What are some things your church would be able to do?

Equipping

Practical steps I can take

1. Study the membership and baptisms for your church during the last ten years. Make one graph for each. Is the membership growing, declining, or plateaued? Are baptisms growing, declining, or plateaued? What reasons can you give for each?

2. Using the demographic information answer the question "Who is your neighbor?" Draw, as best you can, a profile of the typical person that lives in your neighborhood. Make sure you considerer age, household, lifestyle, employment, ethnicity, etc.

3. Draw a profile of the typical person in your church. This will give you an idea of "Who you are" as a church body.

4. Carefully study the profile in number three above in terms of worship style, theology, evangelistic passion, preaching and ministries of the church.

5. Does what you discovered in the profile of your church (number three and four) match the profile of the people in the community? If not, the church must change to meet the community's needs.

6. As you study your spiritual gifts, determine your passion What small group can you start based on your gifts? Will starting this small group help fulfill the vision, mission and values of your church?

SECTION
four
Mobilizing

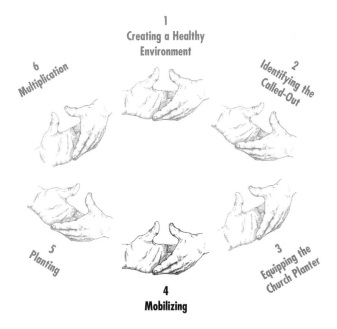

1
Creating a Healthy
Environment

6
Multiplication

2
Identifying the
Called-Out

5
Planting

3
Equipping the
Church Planter

4
Mobilizing

This phase in starting healthy reproducible congregations builds and expands on the three previous phases. Creating a healthy environment started within the walls of the local congregation, but now saturates the recruitment and equipping processes and extends to the mobilization of the church planter. The called-out church planter was initially equipped and now continues to be equipped rapidly through this phase. The mobilization and planting phase may take from twelve to fifteen months. "Support" is the key word for the mobilization phase.

15 Creating a Church Planting Partnership

I said to the nobles, the officials and the rest of the people, "The work is great and extensive and we are separated on the wall far from one another. At whatever place you hear the sound of the trumpet, rally to us there. Our God will fight for us"(Neh. 4:19-20).

*C*hurch planting partnerships are essential in creating an initial support system, not only for the planter, but also for everyone involved in the planting of a new congregation. In essence, a church planting partnership is a trustworthy bridge between the first three and the last three sections of the book.

My definition of a church planting partnership is a diverse group of people representing different churches that meet intentionally to plan for the support, healthy growth, maturity and multiplication of the new congregation. This group meets more often initially and less often once many of the initial goals are completed.

The lead church, other partner churches, local denominational body, state denominational body and national denominational body form the church planting partnership. Each will bring an important contribution to the partnership.

SPIRITUAL PREPARATION

The partners' first task is to pray together. They need to take time for each to share their pilgrimage and how God has led them to this point of supporting a new work. This is a time in which God is refining different personalities and values into one. The basis for the success of the partnership is directly proportional to the amount of time they spend in prayer. The partners specifically need to pray for the selected area. This is probably the most important thing a church planting partnership will do. Remember, that as the partners prepare to invade an area to start a new church, the fiery darts of the enemy are activated. Starting a new congregation is intense spiritual warfare. For this reason, the main purpose of the partnership is to bring unity in order to be able to resist the schemes of the devil. Notice that Nehemiah's first action after hearing about the condition of Jerusalem was to seek the Lord. "When I heard these words, I sat down and wept and mourned for days; and I was fasting and praying before the God of heaven"(Neh. 1:4). After spending quality time with God, Nehemiah began to gather his team together. He painted the picture of the situation and then challenged them to action. "You see the bad situation we are in, that Jerusalem is desolate and its gates burned by fire. Come, let us rebuild the wall of Jerusalem so that we will no longer be a reproach" (Neh. 2:17).

FIELD PREPARATION

The field preparation is normally done before the partnerships come together. Those whom God gave a vision to start a new congregation normally do the field preparation. It may have been a layperson, a pastor or a group of people that are interested in starting the new work. The field preparation consists of getting to know the selected area. Once this information is collected, it is then shared with the partnership. Much of the information can be obtained from the census and other demographical tools. Once the information is gathered, it is wise to verify it by driving around the selected area, taking surveys and talking to people living in that area. These are some questions to answer during the field preparation:

1. Where are other churches in the area?

2. What are other churches doing?

3. Who is your target?

4. Who are the people in the area?

5. What is the education of the people?

6. What is the make up of the household in the area?

7. How mobile are the people?

8. What is the lifestyle of the people in the area?

9. Are there ministry opportunities that the new church can explore?

As the partnership comes together, they can verify and update much of the material gathered during the field preparation.

THE PARTNERSHIP MEETING

In the initial partnership meeting, expectations are shared by all participants. I have found that the basis of disagreements is due to different expectations. Another basis for disagreement results from not determining each partner's financial responsibility. A partner's contribution cannot be measured in terms of dollars only. Many small churches, which are involved in a new church plant themselves, can make an enormous contribution through their practical and technical guidance.

Additional items to be considered by the partnership are the initial goals for the church plant. What is needed in terms of support, field preparations, etc? What are the present and near future (three to six months) needs? Who is responsible for accomplishing a particular task? What commitments are made? Who made the commitments? Remember to write down the dates by which the tasks need to be completed. After the document is finally put in writing, let each partner read it and make any corrections necessary. After all corrections are made, have all partners sign the document. It is assumed that the lead partner will take responsibility for making sure that partners are doing what they agreed to do.

BENEFITS FOR A PARTNERSHIP

The benefits for a partnership are far greater than the tragedy of not having one. Let me mention some of the benefits. First, it strengthens communication among the different people who form a partnership. Second, it keeps all partners accountable. Third, it keeps the commitments made by each partner before the entire group. Fourth, it serves as a timetable to get goals accomplished. Fifth, it helps in securing additional partners. Sixth, it provides an initial plan.

Baptist Convention of New Mexico
Division of Missions Ministries
Dr. Gustavo V. Suárez, Director
Dr. Daniel H. Rupp, Church
Extension Director

New Church: Counterculture Church,
                         Albuquerque

**Church Planting Partners: Central Baptist
                         Association,** Albuquerque

                         Cottonwood Church,
                         Albuquerque (lead partner)

                         Hoffmantown West Church,
                         Albuquerque

Time period: September 1, 2003 –
                         December 31, 2005
                         **(Length of involvement of
                         specific partners may vary)**

The purpose of the partnership agreement is to provide a support system for church planters Paul and Amanda Herzog. The participants in the partnership agreement are representatives from the partner churches, the new church, the state convention and the local association.

Expectations:
1. *Worship experience:* "Whole life worship." Service style will be appropriate for the focus community, as determined by the church planter.

2. *Growth:* A healthy, growing, multiplying church.

3. *Giving:* "Authentic prayer and worship feed each other, then giving comes." While receiving funding assistance from BCNM and NAMB, the new church is expected to contribute 10% of undesignated offerings to Southern Baptist Missions causes. At least 5% of undesignated offerings will go to the Cooperative Program. Church members should be informed about and have opportunity to contribute to the Annie Armstrong Offering for North American Missions.

4. *Participation:* Counterculture Church will offer clear teaching and guidance on "what is a church member." The new church will involve itself in appropriate ways with the Central Baptist Association, the Baptist Convention of New Mexico and the Southern Baptist Convention.

5. *Training:* "Training believers requires intentionality and a systematic approach." Church planters jointly funded by BCNM/NAMB are expected to attend the annual Missions Leadership Conference (every March), one Basic Training for Church Planters, the 2003 Church Planting Conference (Oct. 10-11, 2003) and other training opportunities as offered.

6. *Supervision:* As pastor of Cottonwood Church, the lead partner, Dr. Jack Allen will provide supportive supervision.

Initial Goals:

1. What are the immediate **needs** for this church plant?
   — Equipment: Sound system, video projector, cell phones, etc.
   — Office Space, equipment, & materials
   — Publicity
   — Materials & resources for music & small group ministries

2. What **resources** do we already have? (human, financial, other)
   — Web site on line
   — Some technical equipment
   — Use of worship space
   — Other miscellaneous materials & equipment

   What **resources** do we need?
   — Equipment/services $
   — Publicity $
   — Music/small groups mat'ls $
   — Office space/equipment/mat'ls $
   — Total short term needs: $

3. How do we secure resources in order to meet the needs in #1? (mobilization, marketing, other)
   — Tithes/offerings from Counterculture core group
   — BCNM will provide startup funds for equipment, publicity, materials, etc.
   — Cottonwood Church will provide some startup funds, amount to be determined ASAP

Funding Strategy:
Counterculture Church Planting Partnership

	Monthly	Annualized
Salary/Housing		
Travel		
Operations		
Annuity		
Health Insurance		
Total		

Church Planting Partners	2004	2005*	2006**
Lead Partner Church: Cottonwood, ABQ			
Partner Church: Hoffmantown West, ABQ			
Central Baptist Assoc.			
BCNM/NAMB			
New Church Plant: Counterculture			
Partner Church			
Totals:			

*2005 funding will be reviewed in 2004.
**Funding for the fourth and fifth years will be determined later, according to need, strength of the new church, availability of funds and other factors.

Division of Mission Ministries, BCNM
Church Planting Guidelines

Those serving in a church planting role that are jointly funded by the Baptist Convention of New Mexico (BCNM) and the North American Mission Board (NAMB) in the amount of $800 per month or greater will meet the following guidelines.

Purpose:
1. To provide direction in partnerships between all entities involved in the support of a new church start.
2. To provide a support system for church planters in New Mexico.

Process for Approval:
1. Candidate submits a current professional resume.
2. Personality profile
3. Spiritual Gifts profile
4. Assessment of Church Planter
5. Attendance at the Basic Training for Church Planters
6. Development of a partnership agreement
7. Development of a support system
8. Participation in training events that will further develop the church planter and/or church planting team

Jack Allen, Cottonwood Church, Albuquerque

Hoffmantown West Church, Albuquerque

Paul Herzog, Counterculture Church, Albuquerque

John Torrison, Central Baptist Association

Daniel Rupp, BCNM

Date

REFLECTION

1. What is a church planting partnership? Who makes up the partnership?

2. What is the initial task for the partnership? Do you agree with the author's statement that church planting is spiritual warfare? Explain

3. As you reflect on this chapter, write down your pilgrimage. Where do you see God working in your life today?

4. What would you say is the purpose of the field preparation? What tools are available to you? What are
   some questions to ask?

5. What are two basis for disagreements mentioned in
   this chapter? Do you agree? Why or why not?

6. What are the benefits for a partnership mentioned in
   the chapter?

16 *Understanding Culture*

And Jesus answered and spoke to the lawyers and Pharisees, saying, "Is it lawful to heal on the Sabbath, or not?" But they kept silent. And He took hold of him and healed him and sent him away. And He said to them, "Which one of you will have a son or an ox fall into a well and will not immediately pull him out on a Sabbath day?" (Luke 14: 3-5)

Shortly after I arrived to serve in New Mexico, I received various calls from a pastor fervently complaining about two fellow pastors. He was very upset and insisted that I must deal with the liberal theology that these two pastors were introducing to our churches. After talking to this gentleman for some time, it became evident to me that he had come to value the particular worship style of his church as equal with eternal biblical truth. His primary complaint was that the two pastors were using guitars and encouraging the people to clap their hands.

As the church planter starts a new congregation, it is critical that he has good understanding of the culture of the people group he is planning to reach. So many people I know take culture for granted. Have you not heard a statement such as: "They better learn English because this is America." While I do not argue with the necessity to learn the language spoken in the country, I think that the church planter needs to be sensitive to the customs and language of that culture. It is very easy to distinguish the differences in culture between a Nigerian and someone from the United States. It is much more difficult to differentiate between a baby boomer and a Gen Xer born in the same state. Yet, both have certain unique cultural characteristics, that if ignored, could put at risk winning that person for Christ. As we mentioned in the previous section, it is necessary to keep a balance between the ministries of the local church (who we are) with the needs of the people in the community (who our neighbor is). These four suggestions may help you keep that balance.

BE AWARE OF CULTURE

Many churches form their values and beliefs from a mixture of scriptural truth and the culture from within the church. As years pass, these values and beliefs become traditions that people equate with Biblical truth. Things such as times for worship, Sunday School, clothing and the order of service become "sacred cows." God has blessed the United States much more than many other countries in the world. It is expected for us to have a beautiful building in which we can worship God. However, many people around the world do not enjoy that luxury and consider it an honor to worship under a tree. Some people groups in the world are enjoying a church planting movement of God by starting "house churches." Could that happen here in the United States? I have no doubt that it will happen. The question for us really is, will we LET GO of our traditions and LET GOD do a mighty work through the multiplication of churches that meet in homes? Make a distinction between cultural issues and that which is unchangeable, the Word of God.

PRACTICE FLEXIBILITY

If the new congregation wants to be relevant to the community, it must be willing to practice flexibility. Local congregations can change their practice as long as it does not conflict with Scripture. Recently, some denominations have yielded to outside pressure by ordaining gays and lesbians to the ministry. These practices clearly violate scriptural teaching and are not honored by the Lord. Any group that compromises scriptural teaching can be certain that healthy growth will not take place.

Churches are not able to practice flexibility because they are inwardly focused. Many are the churches that talk about reaching out to the lost. But, a careful inspection of their budget will reveal that a great percentage of it is for inward ministries.

A second reason that churches are not able to practice flexibility is that they are "out of touch" with the community (who our neighbor is). The weakness of being inwardly focused leads to being out of touch. This can be seen in the Christianized language, in the worship styles, selection of hymns and the lack of technology use in the services.

EXAMINE CULTURE

Put every practice of your church through a filter periodically. Examine all ministries of the church and evaluate them to the needs of the community to make certain that the new church is in touch with the people to whom it seeks to minister. Any such investigation will most likely lead to changes. This will complicate things a bit since most people do not like change. This is one reason why many churches today refuse to change and continue to minister with the mentality of the 1950's. Ironically, God requires a change of heart for someone to receive eternal life.

UNDERSTAND THE NEEDS OF THE PEOPLE

One of the ways for a church to be relevant to the lost people to whom it seeks to minister is to associate with them. Get to know them well so that you can understand their hurts, needs and philosophy of life.

Let their culture come into view by hanging out with them. Listen with passion to what they are saying and learn about their interests. Remember this is all about the lost and not you.

Read what they like to read. Look in the community newspaper for activities and who is attending them. What do they like? What places do they go regularly?

Culture does not determine our faith in Christ. But it does determine how we practice our faith. For example, although Cuban churches are changing, most still greet the visitors by waving their hands and not clapping in the church. Be careful to let Scripture determine function, while culture determines form. The latter can change, but the former never changes.

REFLECTION

1. Describe the culture of your church. How does it match the culture outside the church? List similarities. List differences.

2. What are the four suggestions the author makes in this chapter to keep the balance between the church and the needs of the people in the community? Do you agree with these suggestions? What others would you add?

3. What are some "sacred cows" in your church? How did they become scared?

4. What are some customs in your church that are more related to culture than to scriptural truth?

5. What are two reasons why many churches are not able to practice cultural flexibility?

6. What are some things you can do to get a better understanding of the culture of the people in your community?

17 *Knowing Your Target Area and Ministry Focus Group*

To the Jews I became as a Jew, so that I might win Jews; to those that are under the law, as under the Law though not being myself under the law, so that I might win those who are under the law (1 Cor. 9:20).

young, enthusiastic man wanted to start a new church in a certain area of the city in which he lived. His ministry focus group was people between the ages of twenty and thirty years of age. His excitement was soon extinguished, however, when someone told him that the area in which he wanted to start a church had a high concentration of senior adults.

This story illustrates the importance of knowing your contextual environment as well as the ministry focus group you are trying to reach. It is important to understand that the contextual environment and ministry focus group represent two distinct perspectives. The contextual environment takes into account a geographical area that may have many possible ministry focus groups. For example, the area in which you live (contextual environment) may include groups such as Hispanics, African-Americans, Russians, single parents, mobile home park residents and many other possible ministry focus groups that need to be reached with the gospel of Jesus Christ. While every contextual environment and ministry focus group is different, there are reliable princi-ples that will help you know the environment and ministry focus group you are seeking to reach.

One principle is contextualization and it suggests that strategies are determined by the specific context (area and people). For example, the people and the environment and not merely the desire of the church planter, deter-mine the worship style, music and evangelism.

A second principle is the indigenous one. It suggests something that is homegrown rather than imported and therefore foreign to that particular context. The goal in planting healthy, reproducible congregations should be to reach and develop indigenous leaders. Some advantages to this approach are: (a) they know the environment (b) they are more likely to know the different focus group than someone from the outside (c) they are more likely to be accepted by the people in the community (d) they already have a network of friends and family and (e) they are familiar with cultural characteristics of that community.

ADDITIONAL TOOLS

There are additional tools available to the local church and the church planting team that can help them develop a portrait of the contextual environment and ministry focus group they are seeking to reach. Some of these tools are: demographic, psychographic, religious and spiritual surveys, surveys of community leaders, government offi-cials and residents of the community. Use these to create a profile of the people living in the community (see Chapter Fourteen).

DEVELOPING AN UNDERSTANDING OF THE SPIRITUAL CONDITIONS

The church planting team needs to grasp the spiritual thermometer of the people in the community. One way to do this is by doing a spiritual needs survey. This survey doesn't need to be long. As a matter of fact, it is more effective if only a few questions are used. These are some sample questions you may use. (a) What are some of the greatest needs in this community?; (b) In your opinion, why do many of the people in this community not attend church?; (c) If a new church was started in this community, what ministries would they need to offer to help you and your family deal with life's problems?; and (d) If we started a Bible Study to address these issues, would you and your family be interested in attending?

DEVELOPING AN UNDERSTANDING OF THE BARRIERS

The church planting team needs to be attentive to barriers that may be present in the community. These barriers could make it difficult for a new church to be planted.

The image barrier

Churches today have a credibility problem. There is a church in the city in which I live that has a terrible reputation among the people group they are trying to reach. They are known all over town to be people that are always in some type of dispute. Consequently, they have had a difficult time in gaining new members and growing the church.

The language barrier

Some of the people living in your community may speak a different language. In order to effectively penetrate this ministry focus group, the language barrier needs to be torn down. One way to do this is by communicating the gospel in the language of the people and preferably with an indigenous leader, one from within that language group. Acts 10:1-6 and 11:19-21 are examples of people tearing down language barriers.

The cultural barriers

Worship style and the use of various instruments are determined by the cultural make-up of the people in the community. A church planter needs to be careful not to bring cultural baggage to the ministry focus group.

The religious barrier

A church planter recently went to an isolated town to start a new church, only to find himself in the midst of a strong opposition to any church in that area. The denominational office received a call from one of the residents in which he explicitly said, "We moved here to be away from everyone else and I want you to know we will not have a church here." It turned out that there was an active training center for witchcraft in that particular community.

DEVELOPING AN UNDERSTANDING OF THE NEEDS

A church planter team is in a unique position to discover the needs of the people in the community and try to meet those needs. Someone once said: "Find a hurt and heal it and find a need and meet it." As you seek to understand your ministry focus group, there are three needs that must be considered.

Real needs are those clear issues that have created difficult circumstances. These may be physical, emotional, social or spiritual in nature. Felt needs are those needs that are perceived or recognized. There may be some real needs that the individual does not recognize and therefore are not felt needs for that person. Anticipated needs are new needs that develop due to changes in a community. One example of an anticipated need may be neighborhood crime and safety.

DEVELOPING AN UNDERSTANDING OF THE GEOGRAPHIC ISSUES

Church planting teams need to be aware of two types of geographical barriers. Natural barriers such as lakes, rivers and mountains make it difficult for people to interact. Man-made barriers such as interstate highways, businesses, industrial parks and housing patterns also mark divisions between people groups. A pastor wanted to start a church in a new community a few miles from his existing church. He mentioned to me that the people living there were the children of the people he pastored. He added that people in that new community never went back to his area to shop but rather traveled across the interstate for all their shopping. This is a case in which the residents of that new community had more in common with those across the interstate than with their own parents. While they did go across the interstate, we must point out that there was easy access from the community to the areas across the interstate.

DEVELOPING AN UNDERSTANDING OF THE DEMOGRAPHIC ISSUES

The demographic tools were mentioned in previous chapters. By way of review, demographic tools provide information such as: median age, population distribution by age, household size, marital status, education and median income. Population distribution by income, housing type, median housing cost, occupation, mobility and population distribution by ethnicity is also provided through these tools.

DEVELOPING AN UNDERSTANDING OF THE LIFESTYLES [97]

The understanding of lifestyles is very critical to the church planting team. The more you are able to interpret the way of life of the ministry focus group you are trying to reach, the more effective you will be. For illustration purposes, I will describe the people in zip code 33012 in Hialeah, Florida. This area is high density and is projected to grow in the next five years by 2.1%. The racial/ethnic diversity in this area is very low. However, the largest group is Hispanic with 90.3% of the total population. Of these, the majority are Cubans. The family structure is mixed, due to the about average presence of married persons and two parent families. While many graduated from high school, the percentage of those age 25 and above who graduated from college is half of the national average of 24.4%. Some of the real needs in this community are: household below poverty line, adults without a high school diploma, households with a single mother and an unusually high concern about issues such as food, housing and jobs. Based on some of the community needs described above, these ministries are likely to be preferred: (a) divorce recovery program, (b) daycare services, (c) care for the terminally ill and (d) parent training programs. About 85.8% of the households are likely to express a preference for some particular religion tradition. Since this community is predominantly Hispanics and mostly Cubans, one can assume that Catholicism is the preference of most. However, one must balance this fact with the low faith receptivity of this community.

DEVELOPING AN UNDERSTANDING OF THE CHURCH ISSUES

The church planting team should develop an understanding of the environment and ministry focus group in terms of church issues. This will give the team a better understanding of the faith receptivity in that area. It will also paint a picture of denominational preferences or background, how often people attend religious services, spiritual openness of the community and what other evangelical churches are doing in term of reaching the community.

One can get a better picture by exploring the west side of Albuquerque, New Mexico. This is an area that has experienced tremendous growth over the last decade. However, projections for the next five years show a decline of 2.4% in population. The overall diversity in this area is very high. The largest groups represented are Hispanics, with 69.8%, followed by Anglos at 20.9%. However, before one makes a quick assumption about the large population of Hispanics, one should understand that many of these Hispanics are second and third generation and mostly English preference or English dominant (see Chart 1). The most significant group in terms of numbers and comparison to national averages are people between the ages of 21 to 39. The family structure is very non-traditional, due to the below average presence of married persons and two-parent families. The educational level of the residents of this community is low as compared to the national average. The low educational level, although not the only factor, contributes to some community problems such as neighborhood gangs, need for affordable housing and adequate food, abusive relationships, neighborhood crime and safety and social injustice. A significant factor to keep in mind as a new church is planted is that this area is highly resistant to change. Remember that ministry is based on relationships. While the church planter's ideas may be great, as a leader, he is to lead the people in that community with love and understanding of their needs. Church planting is a gradual process which will not happen overnight. The planting team should get to know the people, community, culture and traditions. Pastor them with love and they will cheerfully follow you.

A great majority of the people in this area is likely to express a preference for some particular religious tradition or affiliation. However, this expression does not translate to involvement in the local church. The religious affiliation in this area is very low.

Once the church planting team understands the total picture of the environment and ministry focus group, they are able to develop a contextual strategy to reach the people in that community with the gospel of Christ. And, as you go, remember Paul's words regarding the gospel: "For I am not ashamed of the gospel, for it is the power of God for salvation to everyone who believes, to the Jew first and also to the Greek" (Rom. 1:16). You have nothing more effective in your arsenal than God's holy and infallible Word. One last word of encouragement as you journey along the joyous path of church planting, while the devil emphatically tells you "Give up you cannot do it!" God's eternal voice continues to echo throughout the ages "I will never desert you, nor will I ever forsake you" (Heb. 13:5).

REFLECTION

1. Explain what is meant by contextualization and indigenous. Give examples from your area.

2. What are some advantages of developing indigenous leadership?

3. What are some tools that a church planter can use to develop a portrait of the environment and the ministry focus group?

4. Develop a questionnaire that could be used by your church to explore the spiritual condition of the people.

5. What four barriers related to the community are mentioned in this chapter? Do you see these barriers in your community? Describe what you observe.

6. What are some of the needs in your community? What can you do about each? Your church?

7. Describe your community in terms of demographics, lifestyles, and church issues.

CHAPTER *18* Cultivating the
Community

*Beloved, let us love one another, for love is from God; and every-
one who loves is born of God and knows God. The one who does
not love does not know God, for God is love (1 Jn. 4:7-8).*

While I was a church planter in Buffalo, New
York, I met a newly arrived Vietnamese family.
We soon discovered that we had many things in common.
One of those was the fact that their family and I were
immigrants to this country. We both fled communism and
came to America looking for political freedom. My wife
started weekly English lessons with the family. We
learned about their culture and their pilgrimage. We saw
firsthand the struggle to learn a new language, function
in the midst of a new culture and to live in a totally different climate. As our friendship grew, I met a few other
Vietnamese families. I wanted to reach out to the
Vietnamese community in Buffalo. The churches of the
area had not created an attractive image that would reach
this community. I certainly did not speak their language.
Shortly after God placed a longing in my heart to do
something, He provided me the name of a Vietnamese
friend. I called my friend and asked him to come to
Buffalo and help me reach out to this community. He
accepted my invitation and joined me for a week. As a
Vietnamese, he knew the leadership structure and whom

he needed to visit first. We invited the Vietnamese community to come and view a movie and listen to my friend speak in their own language. I have to admit that I was not ready for what was going to happen. I expected thirty to fifty people to come to this event. God, however, saw things much differently. When the day came, we filled the church to capacity with over two hundred Vietnamese listening to the gospel of Jesus Christ. Some made decisions, but certainly a positive image was established that day, both with the Vietnamese community and their leadership.

Many of the chapters in this book have dealt with the internal and preliminary preparations of the church planter and the team. But this chapter starts a transition in which all that preparation now flourishes face to face with people. If there was one word to summarize this chapter, it would be "image." Whatever the church planting team does or fails to do, will determine the success of the church plant. I would like to suggest media and community events that will help create a positive image in the community.

THE USE OF MEDIA

Many of the new churches started in the last six years have been very successful with direct mail. The success of these churches was related to their understanding of their community and ministry focus group. These churches used various principles that may be helpful. First, the mailing responded to the needs discovered during the time they spent understanding the environment and ministry focus group. Second, they mailed a large number of pieces more than once. One of the new churches started with over two hundred people the first service as a result of visitation, outreach and direct mail. Third, they used the language of the people to communicate effectively. Fourth, they used very colorful and professional looking pieces. Fifth, they expected a positive response and therefore, prepared the people in the new church to generate a positive image in the minds of the visitors.

Contrary to common belief, the use of tracts is a very effective way to create image in the community. Like the direct mailing, the tract provides a way for the people to respond to a specific need. For example, if one of the needs discovered was parenting issues, then the tract should address this need. It is better to focus on one need at a time than give too much information to the people.

A web page promoting the new church can be a great advantage in creating image in the community. Every tract, direct mail, or any other media you are using should point people to your web page. Your web page should be changed frequently to keep people interested. There is nothing more frustrating than visiting a web site and seeing the same information that was there six months previously. Another technological gift is the fax machine. You could send a weekly fax to people and businesses in the community. Include biblical teaching that addresses the needs of your recipients

The use of CDs is very common today. You can add information, not only about the church but also about very positive things happening in the community. This would be a great opportunity to insert biblical teaching that addresses the needs of the people in the community.

Films and videocassette are very effective means of creating a positive image and introducing your church to the community. There are many movies that can address needs in a way that can attract the interests of both adults and children. This approach offers an opportunity to start a Bible study or a discussion group with the people in the community.

Radio and television are also very effective, although very expensive, tools for creating image in the community. However, there are creative ways to deal with this challenge. For example, I had a weekly radio program that I shared with two sister churches in the Washington DC; Maryland and Virginia area. Each week one of us would be responsible for the program and all three churches shared the cost. A friend of mine, also in the same area, bought one minute Monday to Fridays on a radio station before the five o'clock news. He called it "One minute with God." Instead of buying thirty minutes on Sunday he decided he could reach more people during rush hour by purchasing twenty minutes per month. It worked very well for him.

The cost for television is much more than for radio. There are many good opportunities to reach out to the community through cable television. In many cases, some of the times are given as a community service.

While all these methods are effective, I believe that saturating the community with a media blast using a variety of media is much more effective. For example, a church may pick a theme such as "Water of Life." The church may develop "Water of Life" signs that can be displayed in member's yards. You may use the same concept in a tract, radio ad and if you have the budget, even on billboards along the interstate of the community. After some time people would recognize the "Water of Life" theme. There are many other way to use media. Can you think of additional ways to do this?

COMMUNITY EVENTS

The use of media is one method by which a community can be saturated in terms of introducing the new church as well as the gospel. Other effective methods are events that will create additional awareness in the community.

Church members can be part of a recreational league. The church could have as many different sports as there is interest from the people. The purpose is to invite lost people in the community. The leader should be cautious to explain to those that are not part of the church about the expected language and attitude. Bible study, discussion and prayer should be regular ingredients.

Vacation Bible School (VBS) is a way of reaching both children and their parents. A new church probably will not have the personnel to do it alone, but the partner churches can provide sound leadership in this area.

Backyard Bible Clubs are similar to the Vacation Bible Schools except that they are done in members' backyards rather than in the church building. This is an excellent outreach tool that can be done in various part of the community. Partner churches can participate in this initial stage in the birth of a new congregation.

If one of the needs discovered dealt with the family or parenting skills, the new church could provide a series of biblical lessons that would address this particular need. A Christian physician or child psychologist from one of the sister churches could help in this outreach event. Another related event could be a marriage enrichment retreat.

A community outreach event is a great tool for reaching people. The new church can rent a large tent; provide games for the children, face painting, hotdogs, hamburgers, balloons, kite flying and many other attractions. This activity gives freedom to the people in the community to come and go as they please. The only catch would be that in order to participate in the free games and food they must have a coupon. And the only way they can get a coupon is to fill out simple information sheet that gives the church a way to follow up whether by email, telephone or personal visit.

A welcome team could be made up initially of some from the core group of the new church and people from partner churches. They can prepare welcome packets that have information about hospitals, schools, highways, maps of the community, climate, information about the church, purpose, places where Bible studies are being held and other pertinent information. Much of this information can be obtained from the Chamber of Commerce. A personal visit should be made shortly after a new person moves to the community. Information about newcomers can be obtained from utility companies, moving companies, real estate agencies and the telephone company.

These are very important contacts, as many of these people could become part of your new congregation. Remember that church planting is hard work but it is very rewarding to see the lost come to faith and maturity in Christ. The following chapter will provide assistance in the recruitment and training of the core group.

REFLECTION

1. Are there unreached people group in the area where you live? Are you willing to reach out to that community? Do you know someone that speaks the language of that unreached group?

2. What are five principles discussed in this chapter that are attributed to the success of direct mail?

3. Do you use tracts in your community outreach efforts? Do they address the needs of the community you are trying to reach? Why or Why not? Explain.

4. Does your congregation have a web page? Has it been effective in reaching and communicating with your ministry focus area? Is it changed frequently?

5. What other media has your church used? Which one was the most effective? Why? Which one was the least effective? Why?

6. Of the community events mentioned in the chapter, which ones have you experienced? Describe your experiences.

19 *Development of the Core Group*

A woman named Lydia, from the city of Thyatira, a seller of purple fabrics, a worshipper of God, was listening; and the Lord opened her heart to respond to the things spoken by Paul (Acts 16:14).

The church planting team is now at the most critical point in the efforts to start a new congregation. You are beginning to expand the number of people that will help you start the new congregation. The people that will join your team will determine who your next hundred members will be. The core group and the pastoral leadership you will provide will influence the size, shape, personality and future of the new congregation.

DEFINING CORE GROUP

The core group is the initial group of committed believers that come alongside the church planter with the purpose of starting a new healthy reproducible congregation. These are the future members of the church who are being trained for leadership responsibilities. In short, the core group is the new congregation in seed form.

GATHERING THE CORE GROUP

Since gathering the core group is the most critical point in starting a new church, the church planter needs to be very selective in choosing those he invites to be part of the core group. There are various filters the church planter can use in the selection of core group members. One is the vision of the congregation. Where does this congregation see herself in twenty years? A second filter is the values of the new congregation. These are the five to seven unwritten assumptions that guide who we are and what we do. A third filter is the ministry focus group for the new congregation. There are many approaches to gathering the core group; I will offer three for your consideration.

One approach to gathering the core group is to develop the core group from within the ministry focus group. Some advantages to this approach are (a) they know the area and the culture, (b) they care to reach out to friends and relatives from the area, (c) some will be recent converts motivated to learning the Bible and (d) they are already part of a network. However, some disadvantages are to be noted as well; (a) some will be unchurched Christians, (b) others will be dissatisfied Christians and (c) others will be people that like to hop from church to church.

In a recent church start, the planter used a combination of methods in gathering the core group from the ministry focus group. Some members were gathered *one person at a time.* These people were contacts given to the church planting team. The essence of the visit to a Christian was twofold. One, the church planter shared the vision God gave him about the new church. He painted a picture of what this church would look like in the future. Two, the planter explained to this person that, if he became part of the core group, his contributions would benefit the new church start. In the case of a lost person, the visit would be evangelistic in nature.

Another method used by the same planter to gather a core group from within the ministry focus group was by *bringing together a group of people.* This was done through a Bible study group among the ministry focus group. A different approach is to start many Bible study groups simultaneously and then bring them together to form a core group.

A third method used was to gather core group members from a *large group.* This is usually done in the pre-launch of the new church or sometimes in a special community event. Be careful not to let the sight of a large group lead you away from being selective. A large group does not constitute a church. Yet, the selection of the core group will determine the future of the new congregation. Keep your focus on Christ. He spent time in prayer before He selected the twelve disciples.

A second approach is to gather the core group from the partner churches. These would be people who live in the area and presently attend partner churches where the new church is to be planted. This idea was explained earlier in chapter fourteen in the colonizing approach to church planting. This approach will work well if: (a) the new church is going to be ministering to the same type of people as the partner church, (b) the new church is expected to look like the partner churches and (c) the church is near to the partner churches.

A third approach to gathering the core group is a combination of previous approaches. It is wise, when two or more partners are giving people to form a core group, to introduce these people as early as possible in the process.

Some basic principles the church planting team should use in gathering the core group are: (a) have your vision, mission and core values clarified, (b) make "gathering" a continual priority, (c) take advantages of divine encounters, (d) use formal and informal meetings to gather the core group, (e) always leave something printed with people and

(f) ask questions and listen to what the people are saying to you.

DEVELOPING THE CORE GROUP

Keep in mind, as you start the new congregation, that the core group is now part of your immediate family. Therefore, an informal approach is a healthier avenue to communicate, train and nurture this group.

My experience with different core groups illustrates that there is not one perfect day or time to meet. Some groups prefer to meet during weekday evenings in homes. This provides a more relaxed environment. Other core groups prefer to rent a place in which the new church will eventually meet. They use the facilities for special community outreach events and for the development of the core group. This will help the community develop awareness about the new church. Other groups prefer to meet on Sunday morning and give it more of a Sunday School approach. Other church planters have chosen to visit different churches in the area to study other worship styles, ministries, teamwork and other areas that would help in the efforts to start a new congregation. Every core group should meet regularly every week. These meetings should include Bible study and prayer. The planter should always keep before the core group the vision, mission, values and directions for the new congregation. This is a time for spiritual growth, to share life's pilgrimage among the members and to develop fellowship and trust among the group. The planter is moving the core group to be preparing for the first public service. This is a time for intensive training for those that will lead Bible study and small groups ministry, evangelism and outreach programs, discipleship and equipping ministry, community ministries, fellowship ministries and children ministries.

The planter can implement what is described in chapter seven concerning passion, spiritual gifts, personality and assessment follow up with core group members. This will enable the placement of people in relationship to their gifts. The overall objective in the development of core group members is to covenant together to plant the new church.

One question that is often asked is "How large should the core group be"? Our experiences have taught us that the core group should be about twenty percent of your targeted number for your first public service. For example, if you want two hundred people to attend the first public service, your core group should be at least forty people.

CHANGES WITHIN THE CORE GROUP

Healthy churches experience growth but with growth come a series of challenges for the church planter. One of these directly impacts the relationship between the church planter and core group members. As the new congregation starts to grow and more people are added to the church, a struggle can begin to develop among some of the core members. At this point, some make a decision to leave the new congregation they worked so hard to establish. Why? There are three reasons why this happens in every new congregation.

First, there is a loss of intimacy. As more people are added to the church and the membership broadens, intimacy is lost. The pastor must dedicate more time to new people and not as much time to that initial nucleus. Second, core members experience the loss of influence. The leadership base is now enlarged to include other people. As new people are added and trained to positions of responsibilities, the initial core group loses the influence they once had. Third, there is the loss of identity. With time, many of the new "residents" will not recognize the "colonizers," nor will they pay them the respect they deserve for their efforts in starting a new congregation.

The church planter can prepare the core group, but cannot eliminate the certainty of the struggles they will face. He also must prepare himself, as well as the church, for the time when this happens. As difficult as this may be, the church planter should not take this personally. Instead, he should direct the person to a church where he can continue to have a positive impact in the Kingdom. The most important thing the church planter should do is to seek an amicable departure and above all, ensure that Christ is exalted. Let this word be manifested in your life:

> But the fruit of the Spirit is love, joy, peace, patience, kindness, goodness, faithfulness, gentleness, self-control; against such things there is no law. Now those who belong to Christ Jesus have crucified the flesh with its passions and desires (Gal.5:22-23).

REFLECTION

1. Why is the development of the core group the most crucial point in the efforts to start a new congregation? What suggestions would you give to the group with whom you are working?

2. What are three filters suggested in this chapter, which a church planter could use to choose core group members? Do you agree? What other filters would you add?

3. What are three approaches for gathering a core group mentioned in this chapter? What variations are mentioned to the first approach?

4. What are six basic principles a church planter should follow in the selection of the core group?

5. Discuss some basics of core group development? What other things would you add to the list?

6. How will you prepare yourself and the core group for changes that will take place after the launch of the congregation? Why is it important to discuss this issue even as you gather the core group?

Mobilizing

Practical steps I can take

1. Spiritually prepare the partners that will participate in a new church planting effort. Pray together as a group. Pray for the selected area.

2. Take time, as a church planting partnership, for field preparation. Look at chapter fifteen and answer, as a group, the questions under field preparation.

3. As a group, study the culture within each of the partner churches. Make a list and dialogue about those things that are scriptural truth and those that are culture.

4. Examine every ministry of your church and compare that to the need of the community. Is there compatibility? Does anything need to be changed? Why?

5. Develop a profile of your contextual area as described in chapter seventeen. Make sure you are faithful to each step.

6. As you determine ways to create a positive image in your community, prioritize what type of media you will use. What community events will be effective based on your ministry focus group and context?

7. Decide, as partners, which approach for gathering a core group you will use. Write down how you, the church planter, will intentionally recruit and develop your core group.

SECTION five
Planting

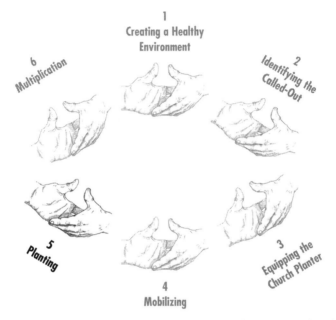

1
Creating a Healthy
Environment

2
Identifying the
Called-Out

3
Equipping the
Church Planter

4
Mobilizing

5
Planting

6
Multiplication

This is a time for "Celebration." Every chapter in this book has been progressing toward the birth of a new healthy and reproducible congregation. There are six stages in the planting of a new congregation. Five of these will be mentioned in this section. Chapter twenty deals with conception, the time when that seed of a new healthy reproducible congregation was planted in your life. Chapter twenty-one discusses the development of that planted seed during the time of gestation. Chapter twenty-two welcomes the birth of a new congregation into the world. Chapter twenty-three illustrates the growth of the new congregation with particular emphasis on the development of leadership. Chapter twenty-four presents the picture of a mature church. The last stage in the planting of a new congregation is reproduction. That will be the topic of section six.

20 *Conception Stage*

A vision appeared to Paul in the night: a man of Macedonia was standing and appealing to him and saying, "Come over to Macedonia and help us" (Acts 16:9).

ongratulations! You have now reached the most rewarding part in church planting. Take a quick look at your accomplishments thus far. There is a positive environment for church planting; you, the church planter, has been identified; there was an initial, but continuous equipping of the church planting team and partners; and some have been mobilized to understand the contextual environment and ministry focus group of the people you are trying to reach. Now, in the conception stage, the church planter must answer four questions that will propel the new congregation to move progressively toward being a healthy reproducible congregation. Hence, the church planter must continually seek to make his spiritual development a priority.

Chart 7

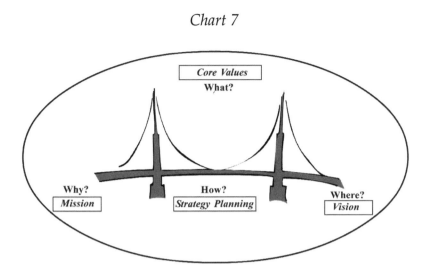

WHERE ARE WE GOING?

The church planter must effectively lead and communicate to others where the new congregation will be in the future. Vision begins with God and not with the church planter or his desire. Nehemiah's vision was a vision from God in response to his prayer (Neh. 1: 4-11). Where are we going? This is the first of four questions we must answer.

DEFINING THE VISION

Malphurs probably has the best definition of vision that I have seen. He says, "An organizational vision is a clear, challenging picture of the future of your ministry as it can and must be."[98] This definition could be dissected for further review.

First, a vision is to be clear. People respond to a vision that is clearly articulated. The planter's role is to continuously describe the picture of that preferred future. I often ask church planters during our basic trainings, "What is the most important part of the puzzle?" Undoubtedly their answer is always "the corner piece." However, I believe the most important part of the puzzle is the picture on the box. By keeping your eyes on that picture, you can finish the puzzle. Second, a vision should be challenging. The vision must stretch the people in the church. Remember, if the vision is of God, it is reasonable to expect that only God can fulfill the vision. It should call people to faith in God. Third, a vision is to be a mental picture. It is to see the finished product, images and pictures of your church in your mind's eye. Kouzes and Posner, speaking from the business perspective said, "The leader's job is to keep the projector focused."[99] Fourth, a vision is to be futuristic. Vision is "being" as opposed to mission, which is "doing." It is a statement of destination and will develop over a period of time. Fifth, a vision should be realistic. It is not only words on a piece of paper that over time can become meaningless. Rather, it is the guiding star toward which the church is moving. The vision is realistic and relevant to the ministry of the church. Sixth, a vision must be pursued with urgency.

Barnabas, Simeon, Lucius of Cyrene, Manaen and Saul were worshiping the Lord, in the church at Antioch. The Holy Spirit said, "Set apart for Me Barnabas and Saul for the work to which I have called them. Then, when they had fasted and prayed and laid their hands on them, they sent them away" (Acts 13:2-3). There was an awareness of the urgency for which God had called Barnabas and Saul. Seventh, a vision is to be motivational. This is the motivational piece the planter can use to motivate and attract people to the church. Eighth, a vision is essential to giving.

People will readily give time, talent and treasure to a clear, challenging, realistic and relevant vision. Ninth, a vision is to be a filter. A vision will filter out ministries and activities that, while good, are not directed toward fulfilling the church's mission. This means that budgeting, calendaring and strategies are all filtered through the church's vision. Tenth, a vision is to be God's specific and unique assignment to the church.[100] It is not unusual to observe church planters who want to duplicate someone else's vision statement as they struggle to write their own. The ornate wording of the document before them confounds them. Nevertheless, the vision statement is God's unique and specific imprint to that particular congregation. Eleventh, vision is to be an empowerment agent. Vision authorizes the people in the new congregation to act upon their piece of the puzzle in pursuit of the total picture (vision).

It is often said that in football, offense sells tickets but the defense wins the game. The church's unique vision is what sells the ticket. The vision is the piece that will attract the people to be involved.

CREATING A VISION STATEMENT

The process of writing a vision statement is time consuming and at times agonizing, but always rewarding once the process is complete. So be very patient as you develop your vision. Remember, it is a process and it will take time. The following suggestions have worked for me.[101]

Take some time and write your answers to the following questions: (a) If God has His way in this place, what will this church be like in twenty years? Think very carefully in terms of the people in the community, an original member of the core group, a young person in the church, city officials and a man leaving the church to start the next church. What would they say the impact of this congregation has been over the last twenty years? (b) How does God want to bless His people and make known His redemptive plan in this church? and (c) Under God, what do I see could/should happen in the life of this church?

After you have answered these three questions, look for words, phrases, ideas, pictures and images that will help identify what God is calling the congregation to be.

Now that you have identified the key words, phrases, images and pictures write a draft statement. This can be done in a series of sentences or an initial statement followed by a series of bullet statements.

Test your vision by putting it through the following filter:

1. Does it glorify God?
2. Does it promote faith rather than fear?
3. Does it motivate people to action?
4. Does it require stepping out on faith?
5. Does it require taking risks?
6. Is this vision right for the time, the place and the people?

Keep in mind that vision is always futuristic. A common mistake in writing a vision is that people normally describe what the church is supposed to be doing. That is a mission statement because it describes "doing." Take a look at the following examples.

Examples of vision statements

New Hope Church will be a community of faith that is family oriented, emphasizes joyful and relevant worship, nurtures a spiritual and inclusive atmosphere, while continually growing through excellence and God-directed risk taking.

The Sanctuary will be a growing group of friends giving themselves away under the direction of the

Holy Spirit to see a global church planting movement initiate from the Greeater Toronto Area.

WHAT DO WE VALUE?

As the Lord was traveling along the road one day, He
turned to one walking with Him and said, "Follow Me."
But he said, "Lord, permit me first to bury my father." But
He said to him, "Allow the dead to bury their own dead;
but as for you, go and proclaim everywhere the kingdom
of God" (Luke 9:59-60). Core values are helpful only if
they can be changed to tangible behaviors. This is the second of four questions that must be addressed.

IDENTIFYING CORE VALUES

Organizational core values are the passionate, foundational, biblical convictions that guide the daily ministries
of the congregation. First, core values awaken your passion. Once these core values are identified, you will not be
able to further reduce them. This becomes the lowest
common denominator that guides your congregation.
Second, core values are foundational. These values form
the basis for developing relationships, ministries, strategies and church systems. One can see the impact of values
in an organization as he reads the programs of the church,
action plan, calendar and budget. Third, core values are
biblical convictions. The real test of a core value is
whether it is biblical. Fourth, core values give direction.
As the new congregation pursues the mission, vision and
strategy, it is the core values that give day-to-day direction to the leadership of the congregation. Fifth, core
values are unwritten assumptions. They are the result of
the sociocultural context within which we were born and
raised. Sixth, core values underlie our words and actions.
Seventh, core values clarify expectations. As the church

planting team shares the organizational values, expectations become clear to everyone. Eighth, core values clarify roles and relationships. Wherever there are people involved, the potential for conflict between roles and relationships increases. Ninth, core values aid in sharpening the mission statement. Your organizational values will be reflected in your mission statement. If you look at Chart 7, you will notice that core values are the total environment where the mission, vision and strategy are carried out. If you were to take core values out of the picture, you would find yourself in the midst of a very disorganized congregation.

CREATING VALUE STATEMENTS

As you begin to develop your organizational core values, please notice two important suggestions. As you begin, state your convictions about how a congregation functions and not doctrinal statements of what the church believes. An example of a congregational value would be participation. How will the values of each person influence the process of leadership recruitment and mobilization? An example of a doctrinal statement is, "We believe in one God."

The following series of activities will help you define your core values. Answer the following questions carefully. (a) What should the church really be doing? (b) How will values impact the way the church carries out its basic functions? Be careful not to confuse the church functions with values. (c) What makes you passionate or for which values are you willing to fight? (d) Where and how do you presently spend your time, energy and resources? (e) If you were free to follow your passion, where would you invest? (f) How does your church want to be known in the community? Start making a list of values as they come to your mind.

Read over the answers you have written to the above questions. Your values of life and church may be found in words or phrases that may be repeated or that may generate an emotional response. Identify the values you see and add them to your list.

Look over all the values you have listed and begin to delete those that are not critical to you. Reduce the number to fifteen. As the numbers are reduced, it will become very difficult for you to choose. When this happens, you know you are going in the right direction. Keep at it!

Now, reduce the list of fifteen to only four to seven. These are your core values. These are additional filters to test your values: (a) If you woke tomorrow with enough money to retire, would you continue to live by these values? (b) If circumstances changed and you were penalized for holding these values, would you still keep them? (c) If you were to enter the corporate world and start a business, what core values would you build into the business, regardless of the type of business?

Use these questions to evaluate your church planting values. (a)Are they behavior oriented? (b) How are the ministries of the church impacted by these core values? (c) Are they true to who you are? (d) Are they value statements or are they doctrinal statements? and (e) Does your list contain between four and seven values?

Take some time to think about how you will communicate the core values to your church planting team, ministry focus group and partner churches. And finally, how do these values reflect the Word of God?

Example of core value
The importance of the family
(Familial)
The growing faith involved in risk taking
(Faithful)
The value of being true to the Bible
(Biblical)
The effectiveness of building relationships
(Relational)
The primacy of doing all things well
(Exceptional)
The excitement of a faith and a church that reproduce
(Reproducible)
The power of being relevant in people's lives
(Useful)

WHY DO WE EXIST?

The mission statement deals with the "doing" of the church. We could look at it this way, if there is a reason for the church's existence, what would that be? Jesus instructed His disciples about their mission. He said, "Do not go in the way of the Gentiles and do not enter any city of the Samaritans; but rather go to the lost sheep of Israel and as you go, preach, saying, 'The kingdom of heaven is at hand'" (Mt. 10:5-7). This is the third of four questions the church planter must answer during the conception stage.

DEFINING MISSION

The church's mission statement is inclusive, reflects direction and biblical mandate for the church. First, it is a statement that communicates, not only direction, but also what the congregation should be doing. Second, the mission statement is inclusive. The mission statement reflects biblical mandate, a part of the church's vision, core values and ministry context. The mission statement should be based on Scriptural truth. Third, the mission statement is vision driven and dictates direction. Fourth, the mission statement should communicate what the church is to be "doing." Fifth, the mission statement is foundational for the planning process. All strategic planning, calendaring and budgeting should be reflective of the mission statement. Sixth, the mission statement builds morale. Seventh, the mission statement sorts out all unproductive activities. Eighth, it reduces frustration. Ninth, the mission statement keeps the church focused on its vision. Tenth, the mission statement is an evaluative tool.

CREATING A MISSION STATEMENT

As you begin to develop your mission statement, you need to consider two different ends of the spectrum. First, you need to know where are you going (vision) Next, you need to know the present condition of the church, core group and community.

As you begin to create your mission statement (a) Identify and list appropriate Scriptures relating to the functions and activities of the church (b) Highlight words, phrases and ideas that make your church unique (c) Develop short, but important phrases to describe your church or ministry (d) Sketch a preliminary mission statement for your church.

Look over your draft and ask yourself; (a) Is your ministry focus group identified in the statement? (b) Does it clarify the need you seek to meet? (c) Does it identify three to five ministry areas? (d) Is it accurate, enduring, concise, memorable and energizing?

The following questions may help you perfect your mission statement. (a) According to the Bible, what should we be doing? Use strong action verbs, not passive verbs, participles, or infinitives. (b) Can the mission statement be understood? What words best communicate the mission? (c) Is the mission statement clear, brief and simple? (d) Is the mission statement unique and specific to your congregation? The mission statement will define how the congregation will divide the large task into smaller, but more manageable tasks, which may take two to three years to complete.

Examples of mission statements

New Hope exists to lead people into *community* with God and His family, to help them to grow to *maturity* in their spiritual lives, to discover their place of *helping* in God's Kingdom and to understand the importance of *sharing* their stories in the world, all in order to experience the genuine *worship* of God.

Sierra Vista Community Church exists to help people know, love and serve Jesus Christ, bonding them into Christian fellowship, equipping them to evangelize and minister to others all for the purpose of glorifying God

HOW ARE WE GOING TO GET THERE?

The previous three questions are foundational for the development of a strategy. In addition, the topics covered in the previous four sections will guide the church planting team in gathering essential information needed in the development of a comprehensive strategy. As you examine chart seven, you will notice that the new congregation, over time, must move toward accomplishing their vision. The core values form the environment in which all of this takes place. The last question the church planter must answer, "How are we going to get there?" will be addressed in this stage. The answers will provide the necessary steps to move forward. The church's systems design brings it all together.

DEFINING CHURCH SYSTEMS DESIGN

Church systems design is a picture of relationships, movement and the results of ministries and systems upon the people of the church. First, the church systems design is a snapshot of the congregation at a given point in time. This may be three, five, or ten years when all the elements of the vision are present and functioning. Second, the church systems design reflects relationships of people and systems. There is a dynamic relationship between evangelism, small groups, worship and other elements of the system. They do not function as ends in themselves, but as part of the entire system. Third, the church systems design is about movement of people within systems and ministries. It explains the point of entry for people, how they move through the systems, how they are assimilated, barriers, back doors, etc. Some questions that may help you better understand the concepts of movement are: (a) What are points or doors of entry? (b) How do people move through the systems? (c) Are there barriers, back doors, or dead ends? (d) How do people move into ministry or exit for missions? Fourth, the church systems design informs about the results of involvement in various systems and ministries. If a person is involved in a small group ministry, what is the result they can anticipate? Fifth, the church systems design includes ministries. These ministries are consistent with the needs of the ministry focus group of the people you are attempting to reach. Sixth, the church systems design includes many systems. Evangelism, small groups, worship, leadership team and discipleship are each subsystems of the church design. Seventh, the church systems design is people. People are the objects of the new congregation. Reaching the lost people in the community becomes the ultimate reason for the existence of any congregation.

CREATING A CHURCH SYSTEMS DESIGN

I believe that the following exercise is the most exhilarating part of the church planting process. It brings every individual piece in the church-planting puzzle, discussed in the first four sections of this book, together as a beautifully functioning and living organism, the Church. Please reflect on the following before you start working on your systems design. (a) Remember the vision, core values and mission statement. How does this system design support the mission of the congregation? Is it in agreement with the core values and vision? (chapter twenty) (b) Consider your context. Does it complement the ministry focus group? (chapter seventeen) (c) Know your strength and weaknesses as supported by your spiritual gifts and personality profile inventories (chapter seven). (d) Consider the following elements of your church: the evangelism strategy, small groups, worship, discipleship/leadership plans, assimilation plans and multiplication plans. Now that you have taken time to reflect and study the suggestions above, you are ready to start diagramming your systems design.

(a) Write each major element on a separate piece of paper (you may use post-it™ notes). Smaller notes may be used to identify various elements of the major component. (b) Place these components onto a large easel pad paper and then consider the following questions.

1. What is the relationship of each component to the other?

2. What is the movement of people into and through these components?

3. Where are the entry points into the church's life?

4. Is the movement of people simple or complex? Keep it simple!

5. Where is multiplication reflected in the system?

Now draw boxes, circles, lines and arrows that indicate the relationship and movement of people into and through the system. (c) Take a look at what you have done thus far. Are there any missing elements? You may add them at the appropriate places. (d) For each major element identified in (a) above make certain of the following:

1. Level of commitment that is required for participation in this component

2. Relationships required to move people from one commitment level to another

(e) Explain how a person from the profile you developed (chapter seventeen) would enter and be connected in the congregation and then move out into ministry and multiplication. The next chapter will provide additional tools for the implementation of the church planting strategy.

Chart 8

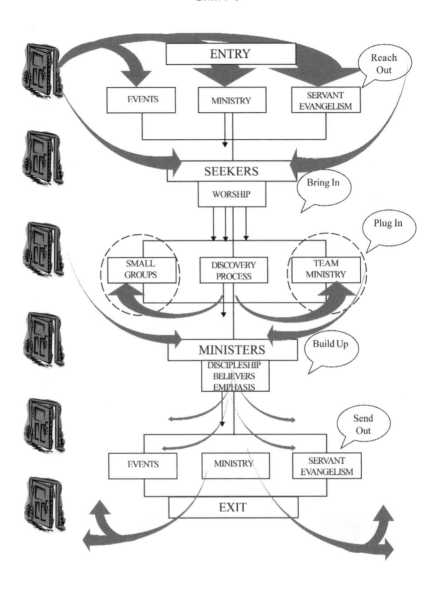

REFLECTION

1. What are the four critical questions mentioned in this chapter?

2. How does Malphurs define vision in this chapter? Share some of your observations about the definition.

3. Why are core values so important? Can different value systems be the cause for strife in the church? Families?

4. What will the mission statement communicate?

5. Study carefully Chart eight, describe what you see in terms of:
   — Ministries
   — Relationships
   — Discipleship
   — Assimilation
   — Multiplication

21 *Development Stage*

I planted, Apollos watered, but God was causing the growth. So then neither the one who plants nor the one who waters is anything, But God who causes the growth (1 Co. 3:6-7).

The church planter now has developed the vision, mission, values and a church systems design. During the development stage, these will continue to be further refined and communicated with the growing and developing core group. Strategies to continue cultivating the community and creating a positive image are accelerated (please review chapter eighteen). The means, by which this work is accomplished at this stage, is through the core group. In that sense, they become the main characters of this chapter (please review chapter nineteen). However, there are many more things that must take place in preparation for the birth of the new congregation. These will be addressed in this chapter.

REGULAR CHECK-UPS
Strategic planning
In our excitement over the birth of a new congregation, we often decide on a start-up date without giving serious consideration to the critical steps that must be taken. When churches are planted prematurely, they often experience years of poor health and struggle.

This section will guide the planter and partner churches in developing a simple strategic plan as they advance toward the delivery date. Identifying and achieving critical markers allow us to determine the progress of the baby. Think of it as traveling the interstate and seeing mile marker 102. You realize that you have come a long way and that you are almost home. We want to distinguish between a critical marker and a marker. Critical markers are few in number. However, should you miss one, the congregation will not be able to start. A marker, however, can be many in numbers. These markers are actions that must be taken in order to get to the critical marker. For example, "gathering the core group" is a critical marker. You cannot start the church without it. Those action steps needed in order to get to the critical marker are called markers.

These are suggestions for preparing the strategic plan. First, markers are the result of action. They should be written in the past tense. Second, markers measure the progress of your church-planting project. Third, when these markers are placed in logical sequence and relationships are established between markers, a strategic plan has been outlined. The detailed actions such as calendaring, assignment of personnel and budgeting must still be worked out. Fourth, both critical markers and markers must be consistent with the vision, values, mission and church systems design. Fifth, they need to be realistic in the time projection. Sixth, there should be a steady progression between markers.

Creating a strategic plan

Work with your core group and partner churches to determine the strategy plan. Think of this as your regular visit to the doctor before the baby is born. (a) Make a list of the markers needed over the next twelve to eighteen months in order to achieve a healthy birth. You may generate as many as fifty to seventy-five markers. (b) Organize your markers in logical sequence on an easel paper. Read again and fill in any gaps or missing tasks. (c) Identify the critical markers and list them. These should be fewer than ten. (d) Organize the critical markers in a process-oriented sequence. (e) Under the critical markers, identify the steps that must be taken in order to accomplish that particular marker. (f) Project a realistic timeline to accomplish the critical milepost. Remember not to rush the development of the church. Your plan should include a time frame of twelve to eighteen months. (g) Identify the selected personnel, budget and other resources needed to achieve each job.

Chart 9

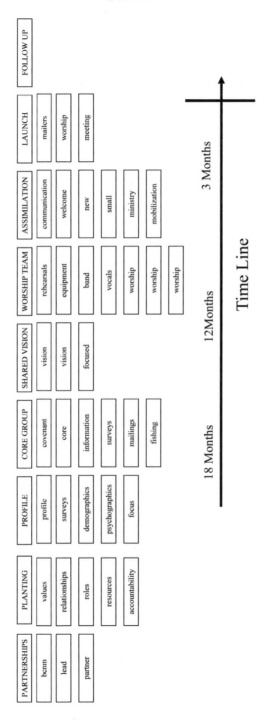

PREPARING FOR A GRAND CELEBRATION

Worship

What style of worship is the best? This has been a hotly debated topic in recent years. Authorities on the subject are found at both ends of the spectrum and everywhere in between. It is not my intent to settle this argument, but to offer different styles that are used today in churches. Ultimately, the question a church planting team and partner must answer is, whom are we trying to reach?

Some think that worship is only for believers. That idea, however, does not line up with the purpose for which Jesus came. "For the Son of Man has come to seek and to save that which was lost" (Luke 19:10). The encounter of Jesus with the Samaritan woman emphasizes her worship experience albeit to an unknown god.

The purpose of the worship service is to facilitate the believers to encounter God in worship and the Word. But, it should give unbelievers a longing for a personal relationship with God. The worship experience should exalt the Savior, edify believers and evangelize the lost.

The believer needs to participate in an environment where the worship experience is God-centered. David's experience is recorded in Psalm 34:1: "I will bless the Lord at all times; His praise shall continually be in my mouth." The unbeliever can also benefit from observing the divine-human encounter in a worship service. The worship experience should also address the edification of believers. In the planning of the worship experience focus should be on the needs of believers. Another essential purpose of worship is to evangelize the unbeliever. The leader should consider the needs and concerns of the unbeliever. Care should be taken not to use words that may be misunderstood by the unbeliever. Plans for worship should include music, language, images, illustrations and drama that are relevant to the unbeliever.

Take advantage of modern technology during the worship experience. Today's generation prefers more visual aids than their parents did. Congregations should consider using audio-visual equipment during their worship. Bring together the music, preaching and audio-visual to communicate effectively with the younger generation.

Preaching should edify the believer and evangelize the lost. The preaching of the Word should be simple enough for a child to understand, yet not simplistic. The sermon should inform but it must also be an instrument of transformation.

There are some elements that could be included in worship. They are not in any specific order, nor will all of them be used at one time. These elements may include; prelude, congregational singing, special music, greeting, offering, message, drama, multimedia, interviews and testimonies, announcements, lighting, visuals, ordinances, prayer and Bible reading.

These questions should be considered: Who should plan the order of worship? In what order will the elements unfold? How much variety will there be from week to week in the elements selected and their order of appearance? Who will give leadership both in planning and leading the worship?

The church planter must consider the context and ministry focus group as he decides what approach is most effective in order to edify believers and evangelize the lost in that community. The particular style is not based on the church planting team's comfort zone, but on the needs of the people in that community.

NAMING THE CHILD
Choosing a name

Do not underestimate the power that there is in a name. Joanne Keating tells the story of her struggles in finding fitting names for her children. She wanted names that would reflect the Irish background of her family. She finally settled on the name, Patrick, since she had an aunt and a sister named Patricia and her husband's name was Patrick. "Easy to remember," she thought. She went into labor and her healthy son was born. She named him Erin Patrick. When her daughter came along, she again agonized about the proper name to give the little one. This time she wanted the name Danica Leigh, since it had power and it could be shortened to form a cute name. She concludes her story with this statement: "So there I was, out with my two beautiful children, Erin and Dani and of course, still trying to explain that Erin was the boy and Dani was the girl. Aaargh"[102]

Remember that churches are made up of people. Whenever you give birth to a new congregation, it displays a unique personality. It has a bank account, a federal identification number, income and expenses. It becomes an individual.

The following suggestions may help you in choosing a name for your new congregation. First, know your community. The new congregation must minister to the people in a specific contextual environment. Therefore, get to know that area well (see chapter seventeen). What names are positive or negative in that community? Can people identify well with that name? Second, be creative. Choose a name that is creative, but that will also communicate with the people in that community. For example, biblical names like "Macedonia" or "Mount Olive" may not mean much to the unbeliever you are trying to reach.

Third, be relevant. Consider the ministry focus group you are trying to reach. If the people you are trying to reach are young, they may not respond to a traditional name such as, "Redeemer Lutheran," "First Baptist," or "St. Andrew Presbyterian." Fourth, be honest. Some church planters, in order to be creative and relevant, have opted to hide their denominational ties. This is unethical and shows lack of integrity on the part of the planter. If there are denominational ties, they should clearly be communicated to the members of the new congregation. Some objections to being tied to a denomination are: "people do not care about denominations," "people do not understand about this particular offering," "people are interested in giving to that which they can readily see."

My responses to these objections are: (a) The planters' responsibility is to communicate why he belongs to that denomination. Paint the picture, through the use of drama, audio-visuals, speakers, etc., of what the particular denomination is doing for people. (b) People may not understand about a particular offering because of a lack of understanding of the denominational ministries. Think for a minute, do the lost people you are trying to reach for Christ understand Christ? No, they do not! Is the cross seeker-sensitive? Absolutely not! "For the word of the cross is foolishness to those who are perishing, but to us who are being saved it is the power of God" (1 Co. 1:18). Are you going to tell them about the grace of God? Yes, that is the reason for the existence of the church. They do not know because no one tells them. So tell them about the denomination and offerings and the lives that are touched around the world and in your own community. Put the faces of people before the members of your congregation. Fifth, be brief. You do not want to choose a name that tells all you believe. A name such as,

"Richmond Sovereign Grace in Jesus Baptist Church," is too long and communicates very little to the people in the community.

Ask yourself these questions, (a) Is it easy to understand? (b) Is the meaning of the name confusing? (c) Is it unique? (d) Is it consistent with Scripture? (e) Will there be a possibility for a nickname? Will this nickname detract from the image the church is trying to create?

Names do communicate something to people. Be careful as you choose the name for your new congregation.

PREPARING THE CHILD'S ROOM
Choosing a location

Choosing a location is equally as important as choosing a name. However, there are various options of places to meet such as: schools (both public and private), colleges, hotel conference rooms, community activity buildings, sharing existing church buildings, portable buildings, club houses, storefronts, restaurants, funeral homes, theaters, recreation centers and large homes. These are some suggestions for the church planter to consider (a) How much can the congregation afford? (b) Does the area (contextual environment) have enough people to support the congregation? (c) Can the structure be remodeled to meet the needs of the congregation and still stay within budget? (d) Will people feel safe as they enter and exit the building? (e) What is the ease of entrance and exit to your location? (f) Is there ample parking space? Will there be a cost for additional spaces? (g) Are there proper signs directing people to your building? (h) Based on your vision, is there room for expansion? (i) Is this a high or low traffic area? What is the implication to the congregation? (j) What are the zoning requirements for this area?

Do not rush to get the first opportunity that is offered to you. Let the Lord direct you to the place He has chosen for your new congregation to meet. God is the one that starts churches. Do not do it in your own strength. "Wait for the Lord; Be strong and let your heart take courage; Yes, wait for the Lord" (Psalm 27:14).

THE PRACTICE RUN
Preview service

The preview service is a way for the new congregation to tell the community they are trying to reach what can be expected once the congregation officially launches. I recommend that congregations hold two to three preview services, at most, before the official launch day. This approach will reap benefits for the new congregation. First, it is a time for the core group to experience a trial run. Second, the core group can study areas that need improvement. Third, it is a way to build a crowd. Fourth, it is a way to add new members to the core group. Fifth, it gives the worship team an opportunity to try out the worship leadership. Sixth, it is a way for the children's workers to observe strengths and weaknesses of their ministry.

The church planting leadership needs to be cautious at this point not to do a large mailing which results in large numbers of people coming to the first preview service. This can be counter productive if the leadership is not prepared for that many people. Also, if more people come to the preview than to the official launch service a shift in the momentum of the congregation may result.

For the preview service, a congregation usually invites a Christian, who is a well known community figure, involved in government, sports, television, etc. This is the high point of the work you have done, hopefully creating a positive image in the community. It is a time to throw out the evangelistic net to appeal to adults, youth and children of the community. Keep in mind that a rule of thumb is that the core group normally makes up twenty percent of the total number of people present at the first service. If you have a core group of forty, you can expect two hundred on launch day. The preview service is the last birth announcement to the community of the pending birth of the new congregation.

REFLECTION

1. What are the critical steps you must take in order for your church plant to become a reality? List them.

2. The worship experience should be God-centered. Study Psalm 34. What is God telling you about worship?

3. What are the key elements of worship?

4. What are some things to consider in determining the name for the church?

5. What are things to consider in determining a location for the church?

6. What is the purpose of a preview service?

22 Birth Stage

Do not be afraid any longer, but go on speaking and do not be silent; for I am with you and no man will attack you in order to harm you, for I have many people in this city (Acts 18:9-10).

 ou have been preparing for nine to twelve months for the birth of a new congregation. Now is the day! You have to admit that your mouth is dry, your stomach is acting up, in short, you are very anxious about the unknown. This is a very normal reaction of the church planting leadership on launch day.

CHOOSING LAUNCH SUNDAY

Choosing a launch day is as important as choosing a name or the location for the church. This was not as important in the 1950's as it is today when most of society is unchurched. Remember that you are trying to reach as many people as you possibly can in the target community. Many unchurched people attend worship services only on holidays such as: Easter, Mother's Day, Father's Day and Christmas. It may be that people are thinking more about spiritual things during these four Sundays. Easter Sunday would be an ideal Sunday to start the new congregation because it is the best attended of the holidays.

There are other Sundays that could be "Special Sundays" in which you may want to start the new congregation. For example, in January you might have a special Sunday highlighting the theme of "New Beginnings." The theme for February could be "God's Love." Your creativity is your only limitation in planning a special Sunday.

There are some Sundays which would be best to avoid. These are those during the "long weekend" vacations such as Independence Day, Labor Day, Super Bowl Sunday and Memorial Day. The weekend in April and October when change is made from or to Daylight Savings time is also not a good time to start a new congregation. The summer months when many families go on vacation would not be good Sundays to start the new church.

PLANNING LAUNCH SUNDAY

You have completed a trial run during your preview services. Now it is time for the real thing. There are three important areas that demand special attention from the church leadership. These are the nursery, parking and the rest rooms. Parents expect the nursery to be clean, safe and staffed with competent caring people. Special efforts need to be used in developing the nursery leadership as well as preparing the room. Ample parking space must be provided. While the churched community may be persistent in looking for a parking space, visitors may not return if it is difficult for them to park. Those related to the new congregation should park farthest from the building to open up the parking spaces closest to the building for the visitors. People expect restrooms to be clean. Just recently, while traveling through a small town, I ran into a friend at a country store. "What are you doing here?," I asked. He said that he usually stops at this store instead of the other one in town because their restrooms are cleaner. This may very well be the deciding factor as to whether a visitor returns to your church.

The message must be a word from God. It needs to be relevant to the felt needs of the people you want to reach. Many choose to preach through a series of three to four messages such as "Reasons to Believe." The series could include messages such as: Can the Bible be Trusted?, Creation: Chance or Choice?, Can I know Right from Wrong? and The Resurrection: Fact or Fiction? Whatever you decide to do, keep in mind that it is the Word of God that produces genuine changes in people's lives. Paul said of the gospel, "it is the power of God for salvation to everyone who believes, to the Jew first and also to the Greek" (Rom. 1:16).

The music must be well-presented. Perhaps a well-known group or professional performer should be invited to this special service. Several factors contribute to the type of music used in the worship service. One is the group you are trying to reach. Two is the cultural background of the people. Many are blessed by the traditional hymns of the past, but the same hymns may not appeal to contemporary, unchurched people. Three is the level of participation you want from the people. Whatever style you choose, keep in mind that the primary goal is to reach the lost and not necessarily to satisfy the believer's preference of music.

The use of drama in the service will not only add variety, but also can complement the message. A four to six minute well-done drama can have a lasting effect in a person's life. Make sure that all the necessary equipment you need for sound is working properly before the service. There is nothing more distracting than trying to fix equipment in the middle of the service.

If you are planning on using a multimedia projector, be certain you purchase one that has enough lumens that allow people to see clearly. Announcements can be displayed before the service. This will allow for more time to worship. In addition, it will prevent announcements that are too long or confusing.

The use of greeters is very important. People like to be welcomed and it is the responsibility of the greeters to welcome visitors to the new congregation. Since this may be the first contact visitors have with the new congregation, make certain the greeters are very relational people. They should know where to direct the visitors and how to make them feel at home. Some greeters could be out in the parking lot, others at the entrance to the building and others along the hallways leading to the worship center.

AFTER THE LAUNCH SERVICE

The birth of a new congregation is something to celebrate. However, the day after that is the first day that growth begins. The church planter and his leadership team must begin immediately building a guest prospect list. This list must continuously be updated. There are many excellent software programs that help the new congregation not only keep track of visitors, but also has templates for welcome letters, baptism letters, members' developmental progress and much more.[103] The first week following the launch service each visitor should receive no fewer than four contacts from the church. Some of these contacts should be done by mail, while at least one should be a personal contact from the pastor.

The assimilation process enables and encourages prospects and visitors to become members and to participate actively in the church (see chapter twenty). You can expect the number that attended the first service to be reduced by forty to fifty percent on the following Sunday. Remember that there is a difference between building a crowd and building a church. While you need to have special events on a regular basis to build a crowd, you also need to pay special attention to the fact that, out of that crowd, you are building a healthy, reproducible congregation. While the church services should be exciting, the congregation must understand that "church" is more than just worshiping. If people get the idea that they go to church only, they will become a mere gathering of people with unmet needs. The church needs a system whereby the people find the niche that leads them to long-term spiritual growth.

The intentional evangelistic efforts and development of the new generation of leaders must be the pastor's primary responsibility. One of the characteristics of a healthy reproducible congregation is the continual development and mobilization of the laity. That is to be the discussion of our next chapter.

REFLECTION

1. Are there Sundays that the unchurched seem to attend worship more often than others? List them. Why do you think this is so? Describe some personal experiences about your church and these Sundays.

2. As you plan for "Launch Sunday," what are three important areas that demand special attention from the church leadership? Do you agree? Why or why not? What are some other important areas you would add?

3. What are important tasks the church planter must do after "Launch Sunday?"

4. The development and mobilization of leaders is an important characteristic of a healthy church. What are some initial steps the church planter can take? In what ways will this lead to the development of new leaders? How can you mobilize these leaders?

23 *Growth Stage*

You therefore, my son, be strong in the grace that is in Christ Jesus. The things which you have heard from me in the presence of many witnesses, entrust these to faithful men who will be able to teach others also (2 Tim 2:1-2).

We are enjoying the many benefits of the technological advances of the past decades. However, those benefits can also be a hindrance for us in ministry. Our society is fast-paced. We are used to communicating through e-mail rather than snail mail. We are comfortable eating at fast food restaurants rather than sitting at the dinner table to eat as a family. We cannot function without our cellular telephones. In short, we want to be in touch with everyone and we want things to happen very quickly.

Developing disciples[104] cannot be a fast paced exercise, but is a rather long and systematic process. It would be equally erroneous to think of discipleship as a program. Jesus saw Peter and Andrew as He walked by the Sea of Galilee and called them. "Follow Me and I will make you fishers of men" (Matt. 4:19). From that time, Jesus spent three years teaching His disciples about evangelism, follow-up, equipping, modeling, supporting and multiplication of ministries. He saw beyond the flaws of that group of twelve he initially selected to the real possibilities of each one.

This chapter is intended to show the developmental stages of people from the time of conversion to the time when they become multiplying leaders. A mentor understands his/her role at each developmental stage. Working with other mentors in your church is essential to producing multiplying leaders.

One of the key characteristics of a healthy reproducible congregation is the training, mobilizing and multiplying of people to do ministries. Ultimately, our goal is to see a multiplying congregation. Speaking about unity in Christ, Paul describes the growth of a person from conversion to multiplying disciple with the ultimate goal of being like Christ.

> Until we all attain to the unity of the faith and of the knowledge of the Son of God, to a mature man, to the measure of the stature which belongs to the fullness of Christ. As a result, we are no longer to be children, tossed here and there by waves and carried about by every wind of doctrine, by the trickery of men, by craftiness in deceitful scheming; but speaking the truth in love, we are to grow up in all aspects into Him who is the head, even Christ (Eph. 4:13-15).

You are laying the foundation for the present and future leadership at this time. Do not be in a hurry.

NON-BELIEVER

The mentor's priority with a non-believer is evangelism. You are trying to present the gospel of Jesus to this person. Paul said, "the word of the cross is foolishness to those who are perishing, but to us who are being saved it is the power of God" (1 Co. 1:18). The cross is the message of the witness. His methodology is building a relationship with the individual. John 4 is probably the best illustration of a witnessing model one finds in the Bible. Jesus builds a relationship as He presents the message to the Samaritan woman. Salvation is all about a relationship and not a religion.

CONVERSION

The mentor's priority is to follow-up with the new believer. His methodology is to provide spiritual food and guidance to the new convert. Paul refers to people at this stage as "infants in Christ" (1 Co. 3:1-3). This is a critical stage in the development of new believers. Many people in churches today never grew beyond this stage. Consequently, they are very limited in what they are able or willing to do. Hence, we have many plateaued and declining churches in America.

FOLLOWER

The mentor's priority at this stage is equipping. His methodology is nurturing the new believer by helping him transition from milk to solid foods. This is the stage where the disciple becomes a "fellow worker." This stage is critical in your responsibility because you are now the "master builder" (1 Co. 3:10). As such, the foundation you are laying must be solid enough that others can continue to build upon it. The materials you use should produce a solid temple that can withstand the fire of God's judgment. Three important areas should be addressed at this stage. First, the believer must understand certain biblical truths so that "you will walk in a manner worthy of the Lord" (Col. 1:9). Paul adds that some results of understanding these biblical truths are that it is pleasing to the Lord, it is bearing fruit in every good work and increasing in the knowledge of God.

Second, the disciple needs to translate this biblical understanding into practical skills. Two examples are found in the gospel of Matthew. Jesus taught the disciples to meet the needs of the people (Mt.14:15-21). The disciples were urging the Lord to send the people back to their homes because it was already late. But Jesus taught them about their responsibility to share and minister to others, "you give them something to eat" (Mt. 14:16). In another example, Jesus taught the disciples a lesson on faith (Mt. 14:22-31). The disciples were in a boat at night, when suddenly Jesus comes toward them. They cried out in fear "It is a ghost!" But Jesus told them, "Take courage, it is I; do not be afraid" (Mt. 14:28). Peter, still doubting, asked Him, "Lord, if it is you, command me to come to you on water." Peter began to walk on the water, but became frightened and started to sink. The Lord taught Peter and the other disciples a very practical lesson about faith. Third, the truth needs to be internalized so that character is transformed. We see this change in character in the life of the apostle Paul. After his conversion, he spent several days with the disciples in Damascus. "and immediately he began to proclaim Jesus in the synagogues, saying, 'He is the Son of God'"(Acts 9:20). What a transformation!

SERVANT

The mentor's priority at this stage of development is to model Christian character for the new believer. His methodology is to show the disciple how to put in practice what he has learned. This is the stage at which a transition is beginning to take place from a follower to a servant. The mentor's role is to model, assist and evaluate the new believer as he performs his tasks. The new believer's role is to serve under the guidance of his mentor. A servant must show commitment to the Lordship of Christ

(Lk. 16:13). The new believer must understand that Jesus is His savior, but now he must make Him Lord of his life. A leader must first be a servant (Lk. 22:26-27) and following Jesus is a prerequisite to service (Jn. 12:26). The apostle Paul said, "Therefore, I exhort you to be imitators of me" (1Co. 4:16). To have a lifestyle that is worthy of imitation is an awesome responsibility-such is the life of a mentor.

CO-LABORER

The new believer has grown and has reached the stage in which he begins his own ministries. The mentor's priority at this developmental stage is one of providing support. His methodology is to provide ministerial experience to the disciple. There is now a natural blending of the role of the disciple and that of the mentor. Paul and Apollos were co-laborers, as were Paul and Timothy. This is a stage best described by Paul when he says:

> So then you are no longer strangers and aliens, but you are fellow citizens with the saints and are of God's household, having been built on the foundation of the apostles and prophets, Christ Jesus Himself being the corner stone, in whom the whole building, being fitted together, is growing into a holy temple in the Lord, in whom you also are being built together into a dwelling of God in the Spirit (Eph. 2:19-22).

MULTIPLYING LEADER

The mentor's priority at this stage is that of multiplication. His methodology is reproduction. This is the time for the mentor to reproduce by sending forth into ministry the person he has been mentoring in order that he may do the same with a new believer. When Paul and

Timothy returned to Ephesus after many years, they found things in a state of confusion. There were a number of false teachers who were causing disruption and conflict within the church. Paul was forced to move to Macedonia, leaving Timothy in charge at Ephesus with the task of ending all false teaching. This is a case where the mentor (Paul) reproduced himself by letting Timothy (disciple) have his own ministry. Timothy, the son of a Jewish woman and a Greek father, had experienced growth from conversion to becoming a multiplying leader. That certainly is our goal.

The following chart shows the developmental stage of a person from unbeliever to multiplying leader. It also points out the priorities and methodologies of the mentor.

Chart Ten

Spiritual Developmental Process

Developmental Stage	Non Believer	Born Again	Follower	Servant	Co-laborer	Multiplying Leader
My priority as a mentor	Evangelism	Follow-up	Equipping	Modeling	Support	Multiplication
Methodology I can use as a mentor	Relationships	Feeding	Nurturing	Showing	Experience	Reproduction
The Word	John 4:7-30 I Cor.2: 2	I Cor.3: 1-3	I Cor.3:10-16	I Cor.4: 16-17 Heb. 6:12 Heb 13:7	Eph. 2:19-22	Col. 2:6-8
Key phrases	"I am lost."	"I know Him."	"I want to learn more."	"I want to serve."	"I want to serve alongside you."	"I need to mentor someone else."

Can you think of someone you can mentor? Pray and ask the Lord to provide someone you could lead to be a multiplying leader.

GROWTH FACTORS

There are some common misconceptions about healthy churches. Some confuse the building for the church. One cannot talk about healthy congregations without referring to the health of people. The church is made up of redeemed people. Another misconception is that bigger is healthier. A larger congregation may not necessarily be a healthier congregation. A congregation that has a full schedule of activities is not necessarily a healthy congregation. So, what makes a congregation healthy?

Mike Regele and Mark Schulz did a survey of congregational development in United States denominations.[105] Their initial hypothesis was that growing churches had a commitment to congregational development and a well-articulated strategic plan. The regional bodies represented in the survey were segmented into three groups. The focused showed the two characteristics named in the hypothesis and several others that supported them. The unfocused, while interested in growth, were less likely to be committed to it. In addition, they were not as likely to have adopted and implemented a strategic plan. The third group was the distracted and they had neither a commitment nor a strategic plan. Regele and Schulz provided an example from respondents in the Presbyterian Church (USA) who indicated, "that they were so distracted by the sexuality debate that they had little time to attend to congregational development."[106] The survey showed that a commitment to growth and an adopted strategic plan influenced other growth factors.[107]

Stephen A. Macchia in, *Becoming a Healthy Church*, presents ten characteristics for healthy growth. Macchia discovered that while everyone participating in the research saw high value in the systems and functions of the local church, it was not the most important. As a matter of fact, the first area of value related to our relationship to God. The second area of value was the relationship to my church family and lastly, how my church ministers and manages.[108] It should be pointed out that, just like the developmental stages from nonbeliever to multiplying leader, growing a healthy congregation is a process. Both require a genuine relationship with God and a relationship with other people before we are ready to minister to others.

Perhaps the one that has best summarized the characteristics of a healthy congregation is Christian A. Schwarz. In his book, *Natural Church Development: A Guide to Eight Essential Qualities of Healthy Churches,* he presents four building blocks that lead to a ten-step implementation. These building blocks ask the questions, "What should we do?", "When should we do it?", "How should we do it?", "Why should we do it?" The uniqueness of his book, in my opinion, is that he has found a very practical way to measure the qualitative growth of a congregation. For years, proponents of the church growth movement have made the assumption that growing congregations are automatically good churches. There are eight principles of healthy congregations Schwarz presents: (1) Empowering leadership, (2) Gift-oriented ministry, (3) Passionate spirituality, (4) Functional structures, (5) Inspiring worship services, (6) Holistic small groups, (7) Need-oriented evangelism and (8) Loving relationships. On the basis of his study, Schwarz is a proponent that a methodology that produces higher quality will generate quantitative growth as a natural by-product.[109] These are three different observations about what makes a healthy congregation. However, the common threads that bind the spiritual developmental process described in Chart ten and the observations of Regele, Macchia and Schwarz are discipleship, delegation and multiplication.

REFLECTION

1. Why is the development of disciples so important? Can you share your personal experience about how you were discipled? How does that compare to Chart 10?

2. Describe the spiritual development process from nonbeliever to multiplying leader. What is your role in this process today?

3. Describe the mentor's priority in each of the steps.

4. Describe the mentor's methodology in each of the steps.

24 *Maturity Stage*

Until we all attain the unity of the faith and of the knowledge of the Son of God, to a mature man, to the measure of the stature which belongs to the fullness of Christ (Eph. 4:13).

This chapter is intended to describe what a healthy and mature congregation would look like. It is difficult to pinpoint, in describing the stages of church planting, when one stage ends and another stage begins. Instead, one stage blends with another stage. Growth continues to happen both spiritually and numerically. The congregation is now weaning herself from partner churches, ministries are expanding and the congregation is developing additional ministries. One may ask the question, "What makes a mature church?" A mature congregation reflects healthy characteristics, intentional leadership and plans to multiply herself.

HEALTHY CHARACTERISTICS OF A MATURE CONGREGATION

Spiritual passion

The first chapter of this book sets the foundational truth that only spiritually healthy people can start healthy reproducible congregations. So it should be no surprise that spiritual passion is a key ingredient of a mature congregation. This passion is expressed in the way their faith is lived out with commitment, fire and enthusiasm. Prayer life, Bible reading and Bible study are some factors influencing the spiritual life of an individual.

Biblical conviction

Mature churches that consistently reach the lost, hold to a high view of Scripture. These are churches that have a conviction, not only about the need for salvation, but also about the fact that every person without Christ is lost and condemned. These beliefs give birth to other Biblical truths such as the divine inspiration of Scripture, sin, salvation, grace, repentance, faith and adoption.

Relationships

Chapter four mentions the need for relational theology as you approach the task of church planting. W. Oscar Thompson, Jr., in his book, *Concentric Circles of Concern*, teaches about a relational style of evangelism. Thompson's concentric circle is made up of seven circles, like a target with a bull's eye in the center. The inner most circle is self. This points to the need of everyone to have a right vertical relationship. It is this relationship with Christ that brings about change in self. Only then can we proceed to reach out effectively across the circle. The other circles are immediate family, relatives, close friends, neighbors or business associates, acquaintances and person X.

The Bible teaches about the relational aspect of evangelism. Acts 20:20 tell us that they went from "house to house." Andrew found his brother Simon (Jn. 1:40-41), Jesus found Philip (Jn. 1:43), Philip found Nathanael (Jn. 1:45), the woman at the well went back to her city (Jn. 4:28) and Cornelius gathered his relatives and close friends (Acts 10:24). It is a very natural way of sharing the gospel with others. Some other relational aspects of a mature congregation are: the time that members spend with one another outside church sponsored events, laughter in the church and pastoral knowledge of personal problems within the membership.

Small groups

Mature and healthy congregations have developed small groups where Christians can find intimate community, practical help and intensive spiritual interaction. These groups go beyond discussion of Bible texts to the application of biblical truth to the everyday issues of their lives. Small groups are where people learn to serve others. Growing congregations actively promote the multiplication of small groups.

Evangelism

How shall they hear without a preacher? (Rom. 10:14) Any mature and healthy congregation makes evangelism a priority. Every believer has a mandate to evangelize the lost. "Go therefore and make disciples of all the nations. . ." (Matt. 28:19). It is, therefore, the task of every Christian to serve non-Christians, communicate clearly the gospel and to put them in contact with a local congregation.

Lay mobilization

Mature churches do an effective work of unleashing the lay people in their congregations. They provide discipleship (growing believers from conversion to multiplying leaders), delegation (they are constantly training and placing believers in positions of responsibility) and multiplication (their goal is to reproduce leadership at all levels). The leadership equips, supports, motivates and mentors individuals to enable them to become all that God wants them to be.

Gift-oriented ministries

We are so familiar with nominating committees that are more concerned about filling a vacancy than they are in matching the position with the right spiritual gifts. The role of the leadership of the church is to help people discover their spiritual gifts and to place them in the right ministries. Ephesians 4:11-12 offers an interesting insight for us which is often overlooked by many people in our churches. All the gifts mentioned in verse eleven are for *equipping* the saints, for *work* of service and for the *building up* of the body of Christ. There is a natural progression that moves from equipping to ministries, resulting in the body of Christ being effective and mature. When a congregation focuses inward, it suggests that the body of Christ is not functioning according to their gifts.

Many believers are involved in ministries where they are not gifted. This brings a sense of frustration and sometimes defeat. Can you imagine what would happen to a church where people serve in areas where they are gifted? Certainly there would be joy in ministry. This is one reason why we give emphasis to utilizing the temperament and gifts inventory of prospective church planters as explained in chapter seven.

INTENTIONAL LEADERSHIP

God calls individuals to positions of both spiritual and political leadership. Such leadership requires the carrying of responsibilities toward both God and his people and is to be exercised with humility. This called leadership is strategic in the growth of congregations. Jesus Christ gave leadership of the church to the apostles, who in turn appointed leaders in the churches they founded (Acts 4:34-35). Sin is no respecter of persons, therefore Paul's advice to leaders is, "be on guard for yourselves and for all the flock, among which the Holy Spirit has made you overseers, to shepherd the church of God which He purchased with His own blood" (Acts 20:28). Jesus Christ described the perils from the failure of spiritual leaders (Matt. 23:4-36). He wants to see a spirit of servanthood among the people He called to leadership (Mk. 10:42-45).

Characteristics of leaders

Many studies have been done over the years in order to identify the key traits or characteristics one would like to have in their supervisors. Kouzes and Posner, in their research, have identified four desirable characteristics: honesty, competence, forward-looking and inspiring.[110]

Honesty involves trusting the leader enough to follow him. Integrity is measured by the commitment, actions and follow-through of the leader. Consistency between beliefs and action is another measuring tool. A New York Times/CBS poll taken in 1985 showed that only thirty-two percent of the public believed that corporate executives were honest. Unfortunately, nearly twenty years later, recent events involving corporate America have probably contributed to a further erosion of this trust.

Competence becomes the antidote to seeds of doubts. It is difficult to follow someone when doubts about that person's competence exist. People in congregational leadership positions must exhibit expertise in their particular area of ministry. A Sunday School teacher should demonstrate proficiency in handling the Word of God and teaching methodologies.

A visionary leader needs to understand and clearly articulate to others where he is leading the congregation. He must be able, not only to visualize the future of the new congregation, but to communicate that vision as well. Without a forward-looking path he will only lead others to remain static or to wander without a clear destination. This type of leadership brings about frustration and an attitude of pessimism.

Inspiring leadership provides passion for a cause. The leader becomes a player-coach. As such, he provides direction and encouragement, but is also a participant in the accomplishment of the congregational goals. The passion from the inspiring leader ignites the eagerness of followers to get on board.

Leadership practices

Leaders are pacesetters. They like to step out into unknown territories and take risks in order to discover creative and effective ways of doing ministries that will reach a lost world for Christ. Leaders look at the future like an architect looks at blueprints. It is that image in the mind of a leader that pulls him forward to that goal. However, as I mentioned in chapter twenty, that image or vision of the future needs to be clearly articulated if it is to become a shared vision. Nehemiah was successful in sharing his vision because he knew the immediate needs of the people and had their interest at heart.

Nehemiah was an effective leader because he made it possible for others to participate. His plan was not about "me," but it was about "us." He created an atmosphere of trust and human dignity. The people rebuilding the broken down walls of Jerusalem felt strengthened by their leader. He worked to build a team with depth beyond the leadership.

The leader of a new congregation must model the way by leading out in the development of the vision, mission and values for the new congregation. Leaders create standards of excellence and then set examples for others to follow. Nehemiah shared his vision for rebuilding the wall and for the spiritual renewal of the people. He did not quit during the difficult times, but rather he was determined to accomplish what he had started. He told those who mocked him, "The God of heaven will give us success; therefore we His servants will arise and build . . ." (Neh. 2:20).

Leaders encourage the heart of their people. They create and celebrate the small victories. A leader must recognize contributions in order to keep hope and determination alive. Nehemiah realized that the work was great and extensive and that the separation among the workers was great (Neh. 4:19) and he also saw the toxic seed of discouragement setting into the lives of the people. "The strength of the burden bearers is failing, yet there is much rubbish; and we ourselves are unable to rebuild the wall" (Neh. 4:10). Nehemiah, the leader, came and spoke to the nobles, the officials and the rest of the people "do not be afraid of them; remember the Lord who is great and awesome and fight for your brothers, your sons, your daughters, your wives and your houses" (Neh. 4:14).

PLANS FOR MULTIPLICATION

Any healthy and mature congregation makes intentional plans for multiplication. Reproduction can happen by chance or as a result of planning. Those that are planned usually bring better results and less adjustment. There are costs to both spiritual and physical parenthood in terms of self-sacrifice, tears and commitment to prayer.

Intentional planning

The pastor and leaders of the lead partner-to-be congregation, must be intentional in their plans to multiply. At this stage, the congregation should be putting into practice four of the six sections of the book. These are (a) creating a healthy environment, (b) identifying the called-out one, (c) equipping both the planter and the people of the partner congregation and (d) mobilization of lay people for church planting. As you can readily notice, these four steps in the process are the first four sections of the book (chapters 1-19). The cycle from starting a church to becoming a multiplier congregation is almost complete. Reproduction should be the goal of every healthy congregation.

Inclusive planning

Planting new congregations needs to include as many people as possible. Some may open their homes for a Bible study or Vacation Bible School during the summer, while others may feel led to teach the Bible or lead singing or care for children during Bible studies. Others may feel comfortable going house to house passing out tracts or information about the new congregation. The point is that there is a place for everyone in the start of a new congregation. In addition to people, who are the most valuable resources, the church depends on the support of the regional and state denominational bodies. It is indeed a partnership of people who work as a team in order to plant a new church.

Intelligent planning

Multiplication is not about working harder, but about working smarter. Moses was used greatly by God to deliver Israel from the hands of Pharaoh and the Egyptians. "Moses sat to judge the people and the people stood about Moses from the morning until the evening" (Ex. 18:12). Moses was working very hard, but not necessarily very smart. Jethro, Moses' father-in-law, suggested a better way of counseling the people coming to him.

You be the people's representative before God and you bring the dispute to God, then teach them the statutes and the laws and make known to them the way in which they are to walk and the work they are to do. Furthermore, you shall select out of all the people able men who fear God, men of truth, those who hate dishonest gain; and you shall place these over them as leaders of thousands, of hundreds, of fifties and of tens" (Exodus 18:19-21).

This multiplication principle, which is the key for effective evangelism, is seen in a person's network of family, friends, colleagues, etc. Everyone that comes to faith in Christ lives in a network of relationships to a group of non-Christians. When a new congregation sees these bridges, a multiplication process is initiated.[111]

Planning for a new congregation takes time and much hard work. Remember to be intentional, inclusive and intelligent in your planning. Use the relationship network you have available to make this experience a successful one. The next section will discuss multiplication, the last step in the church planting process.

REFLECTION

1. Name and describe the healthy characteristics of a mature congregation.

2. How is spiritual passion expressed in your life?

3. Why is biblical conviction an important characteristic of a mature congregation? How do you see this communicated in your church?

4. Why is relationship so important in ministry? How relational are you? Can you identify barriers that keep you from being relational? What factors contribute to you being relational?

5. How effective is your church in training and mobilizing the laity? How can the mobilization of lay people be intensified?

Planting

Practical steps I can take

1. As the church planter for a new congregation, work on creating a vision statement. Follow the suggestions under "creating a vision."

2. Define the core values for the new congregation. Follow the suggestions under "creating value statements."

3. Create the mission statement for the new congregation. Follow the suggestions under "creating a mission statement."

4. Creating a church planting system design will allow you to see the picture of relationships, movements and results of ministries and systems of people in the congregation. Create a church systems design by following the suggestions under "creating a church systems design."

5. As you work with your core group, determine the things that are critical in order to start the new congregation. Follow the suggestions under "creating a strategic plan."

6. Determine a name for the new congregation.

7. Review the spiritual developmental process and the role you play as a mentor. Write down the names of five people that need to hear the gospel today.

8. Review the healthy characteristics of a mature congregation discussed in chapter twenty-four. Does your plan for the new congregation match the healthy characteristics? Explain

9. Write down specific plans you have for starting new congregations.

SECTION Six
Multiplication

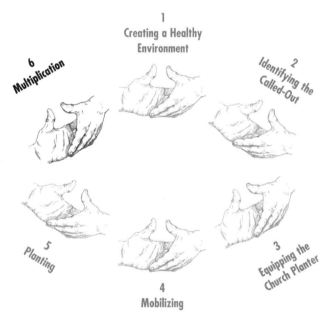

1
Creating a Healthy
Environment

6
Multiplication

2
Identifying the
Called-Out

5
Planting

3
Equipping the
Church Planter

4
Mobilizing

This section challenges the reader to go beyond planting a new congregation to planting reproducible congregations. One deals with adding new congregations while the other deals with multiplication. For example, if one congregation starts a new church every two years, the result would be four churches in six years. But, if that same congregation determines to start a new reproducible congregation every two years, there would be seven congregations in six years. In the same period the number of churches double when multiplication becomes a factor. If you extend the period of time to eight years the difference would be five if adding and eleven if multiplying. The multiplication factor is not only explosive, but biblical. The key word for this section is "reproduction."

Multiplying Congregations

But there were some of them, men of Cyprus and Cyrene, who came to Antioch and began speaking to the Greeks also, preaching the Lord Jesus (Acts 11:20).

We live in a multicultural world. In the block where I live, the neighbor to my right is from California the one to my left from Spain, across the street from Vietnam and a lady that lives down my street is from Korea. The experience of the first century church was very similar to our world today. One of the first cross-cultural events is recorded in Acts 10. Cornelius, a gentile, gathered his relatives and close friends to hear the gospel from the mouth of Peter, a Jew. As a matter of fact, it did not take long for Peter to mention in his sermon, "I must certainly understand now that God is not one to show partiality but in every nation the man who fears Him and does what is right is welcome to Him" (Acts 10:34-35).

BIBLICAL EXAMPLE

The church at Antioch is an example of a multiplying congregation. However, what happened at Antioch started with the persecution that arose as a result of Stephen's death (Acts 8:1). The Hellenists[112] were driven out of Jerusalem. This persecution took the Hellenists in many different directions as they started new congregations. It is important to see the emphasis they placed on evangelizing specific people groups. First, they shared the Gospel with the Jews. ". . .made their way to Phoenicia and Cyprus and Antioch, speaking the word to no one except to Jews alone" (Acts 11:19). This suggests that the Hellenists, Jews themselves, went to evangelize and plant churches among the Jewish people in these three cities. Perhaps these people were Hellenists like the missionaries while others were Jewish. At any rate, they would have been able to share the gospel without a great many evangelistic barriers. "But there were some of them, men of Cyprus and Cyrene, who came to Antioch and began speaking to the Greeks also . . ." (Acts 11:20). Second, they shared the gospel with the Greeks. This verse presents a cross-cultural ministry between the Hellenists and the Gentiles. The Lucius of Cyrene described in Acts 13:1 may have been this man. Barnabas was from Cyprus (Acts 4:36) and later became involved in this ministry.

Peter Wagner suggests that there were two missionary efforts. The first one is described in verse 19. The second missionary effort was that of the established churches in Cyprus and Cyrene sending missionaries to establish churches among the Gentiles in Antioch (Acts 19:20). He believes that there were probably eight and ten years between the two missions.[113]

When Paul and Barnabas arrived in Salamis, they set a strategic pattern for most of Paul's subsequent evangelistic trips. Paul normally first went to the population centers. He sought a synagogue as the first place to preach the gospel. He had a strategic reason for doing this. There were three types of people that were part of a synagogue. (a) Jews who could trace their ancestry to Abraham, (b) Proselytes who were born Gentiles, but who chose to convert and to become Jews instead and (c) God-fearers, who were also born Gentiles, but who chose to maintain their Gentile identity while associating with the synagogue as best they could, so they could follow Jehovah God.[114]

Paul and Barnabas established churches in Iconium, Lystra and Derbe and many other cities. They were not well received, as was often the case. The ethnic Jews were at the forefront of the riots and attacks on missionaries. After Paul was left for dead at Lystra, He and Barnabas continued to Derbe. They went on to win a large number of disciples in that city (Acts 14:21). They then returned to Lystra, Iconium and Antioch "strengthening the souls of the disciples, encouraging them to continue in the faith and saying, 'through many tribulations we must enter the Kingdom of God'" (Acts 14:22) and appointed elders at each church. They concluded their first missionary journey with a furlough in Antioch where they gathered the church and reported all the great things the Lord has done.

Many of the churches which were started by the missionaries from the church at Antioch were multiplying themselves. It is difficult for many of us to think of these churches as "house churches" because of our preconceived ideas. It is probably just as difficult for denominations to look at a movement of house churches because they fear loss of control of those groups. The question we must settle is, whether we want church planting growth that we can control or do we want a movement of God, which we cannot control? We cannot have it both ways. Personally, I want to see God bring about a movement of healthy reproducible congregations that will saturate communities, win the lost, gather believers into strong, reproducible congregations and multiply. Dean S. Gilliland, referring to the church at Antioch said, "The most important feature of the church was the multitude of small units, each of which met together, working out its new life in sharing blessings and working through problems. It is an error to think even of Paul's urban churches as large single congregations."[115]

There are many instances in which Paul speaks of house churches. He sends greetings to the church that meets at Priscilla and Aquila's house. (Rom. 16:5; 1 Co. 16:19), to the church that meets at Nympha's house (Col. 4:15) and to Apphia and Archipus and to the church in your house (Philem. 1:2). Lydia, from the city of Thyatira, was listening to Paul and the "Lord opened her heart to respond" (Acts 16:14). It is obvious the Lord worked in her life through her baptism and that of her household. This is further evidenced by her willingness to open her home for a place of worship (Acts 16:40).

Antioch was a multicultural and multi-linguistic city of about 500,000 people. Like many large cities, Antioch was a blend of religious beliefs. Nearby was a cult center for the Greek goddess, Daphne. This cult deteriorated into the practice of sacred prostitution. Antioch was infamous throughout the Roman Empire for its immorality. A characteristic statement about the degenerating morality of Rome is that of Juvenal, a satirist of the time, who made the observation that the "filth of the Orontes" had flown into the Tiber.[116] The Jewish community numbered between 25,000 and 50,000 people.[117] Like most cities of our day, people are inclined to live in communities with the same people group. Paul saw a large Gentile population in Antioch which he could reach with the gospel. This is of missiological significance to our present day ministries. Paul's missionary strategy was to target specific people groups with the gospel. His sermon which is recorded in Acts 13:16, gives us an example of "contextualization." In other words, Paul is addressing people groups in a way that would readily identify them "Men of Israel" are Jews, including proselytes, who keep the law, circumcise their male children and strictly maintain a kosher kitchen. "You who fear God" are uncircumcised Gentiles who are attracted to the synagogue community and to God, but who have remained Gentiles and who have not promised to keep the whole law.[118] In verse 26 Paul presents a gospel that is for all people, Jews and Gentiles alike. "Brethren, sons of Abraham's family and those among you who fear God, to us the message of this salvation has been sent" (Acts 13:26).

It is God's intent that all healthy things would reproduce. The church of the first century was not different. They had a passion from God to not only start new churches, but that those would become healthy and multiply.

MODERN DAY EXAMPLE —
THE SANCTUARY, OAKVILLE

Jeff and Laura Christopherson moved to the Greater Toronto Area (GTA) from western Canada to plant a new church. The population of the GTA is 5.3 million, an urban sprawl that spans many Canadian cities. When Jeff and four other families began the process of starting the new church, in 2000, the Lord told him three things, (a) Trust me and I will take care of you, (b) I'm going to do an incredible work and (c) Don't try to steal my glory. "It is a privilege to start something from scratch," said Jeff. The Sanctuary vision is to reach Canada by planting reproducible churches. Their vision statement is, "A growing group of friends giving themselves away under the direction of the Holy Spirit to see a global church planting movement initiate from the Greater Toronto Area." Toronto is the financial center of Canada and the leaders of Toronto live in Oakville, a suburb of the GTA. The first church was planted at Oakville with the idea that reaching the "influencers" will allow the church to plant other churches.

The name Sanctuary was carefully chosen to strike a balance between 'grace' and 'truth' (see John 1:14). The image of 'sanctuary' reminds people of a safe haven – this is the 'grace' component. The word 'sanctuary' is an Old Testament image representing the presence of God-this is the 'truth' component. Jeff sees a spirit of interdependence, in the book of Acts. He sees a balance between the autonomy of the local church and the network of churches Paul was starting. Paul did not have a problem telling churches to "shape up." They needed each other. Jeff often wonders what a first century church would look like in the 21st century. While he does not yet have all the answers, Jeff believes that three essential ingredients are team spirit, faith and an interdependent spirit. Two professional members of the Sanctuary have resigned their jobs to become part of a new church start. People in the first century were joining a movement. "And some of them were persuaded and joined Paul and Silas, along with a large number of the God-fearing Greeks and a number of the leading women" (Acts 17:4).

The Sanctuary had their first service on September 9, 2001. That first year they baptized 53 people and expect to do the same the second year. God called Christopherson, the senior pastor, to plant 25 church planting centers by the year 2020. In less than two years, this congregation of about three hundred people has already started five church planting centers. Some church planters have been rejected because they are interested in starting megachurches. All the people who have joined have come without any salary or any promise of receiving one. They have also signed a covenant to start reproducing church planting centers, not just churches. These church planting centers exist to train leaders to reproduce by starting new church planting centers and carrying out the vision of the Sanctuary. A church chooses whether to gather or to give away. "Most churches gather-but that's when they stop multiplying and start adding," says Christopherson.

REFLECTION

1. In a Bible dictionary, study the background information of the term "Hellenist."

2. Describe Paul's strategic reasons for visiting the synagogues upon his arrival to a new city.

3. Do a study of the house-church concept on the internet. Research what various denominations are doing on the subject. Study the book of Acts and specifically look for the house-church concept.

4. Study Paul's sermon in Acts 13:16. Paul is addressing specific people groups with the gospel. Can you identify the groups he is addressing? Can you compare that to your present ministry?

26 *The American Mosaic*

Now there were Jews living in Jerusalem, devout men from every nation under heaven (Acts 2:5).

America is not a melting pot, but a stew. America is a nation with approximately 500 ethnic groups speaking 636 languages. America is a nation of many nations. Each of these groups is distinct from the other and each likes to maintain their own cultural identity. America is home to the Cuban who likes to worship in his own language and among his own people and eat black beans and rice. America is home to the Italian who likes to worship in his own language and among his own people and eat lasagna, spaghetti and meatballs. America is home to the Laotian who likes to worship in his own language and among his own people and eat sweet rice and fruits. It is roughly estimated that North America (United States and Canada) has 220 million people that have never heard the gospel.[119] You do not have to travel to the Far East or Africa to seek the lost. You may only have to go across the street or to the next room. America is a nation of many nations!

God, in His wisdom, is bringing the world to America. The Statue of Liberty has welcomed immigrants from the entire world to this country. Her inscription reads:

Give me your tired, your poor,
your huddled masses yearning
to breathe free, the wretched refuse
of your teeming shore.[120]

and it stands for freedom from political oppression. The cross of Jesus Christ stands for freedom from the oppression of sin. I know first hand because I received political freedom in 1963 and I received spiritual freedom in 1978.

A NEED FOR CHRIST [121]

1. There are an estimated 1.3 million abortions per year in the United States. 22 percent of all pregnancies end in abortion. Half of all pregnancies in unmarried women end in abortion.

2. A third of all births are to unmarried women.

3. There are over 30,000 suicides each year in the United States.

4. There are 1.1 million divorces each year in the United States.

5. There are in excess of 40,000 porn sites on the World Wide Web. According to U.S. News, Web surfers spent a billion dollars to access pornographic sites.

6. There are 32.2 million people living in poverty in the United States. That is 11.8 percent of the total population.

7. There are 1.4 million prisoners under federal or state jurisdiction.

8. An estimated 14.8 million Americans use illicit drugs.

These statistics reveal the spiritual and moral decay in North America. Alcoholism, drug abuse, teen pregnancy, abortion, homosexuality, school violence, child abuse, pornography, rape and murder permeate our nation. George Washington said, "It is impossible to rightly govern the world without God and the Bible." Spiritual decline leads to moral decay. America is incrementally and systematically rejecting God. We have an incredible opportunity to reach the world by starting new healthy reproducible congregations among its many diverse people groups.

THE POPULATION IS GROWING [122]

In the last ten years, the United States added 33 million people to its population. This is the largest increase of any decade in history. 1.7 million people moved into the United States between 1999 and 2000. Almost two thirds of these were foreign-born and not United States citizens. Most moved into the South and West. There is evidence that the nuclear family is changing. This is another indication of the moral decay of our times. Families represented 81 percent of the households, in 1970, but only 69 percent of households in 2000. The decline in the proportion of married-couple families with children under age 18 was especially evident, falling from 40 percent of all households in 1970 to 24 percent in 2000.

The population grew by 13 percent in the 90's. This growth occurred primarily to the West and the South. Metropolitan areas grew faster than nonmetropolitan areas, 14 percent and 10 percent respectively. The median age of the population in 2000 was 35.3 years, the highest it has ever been. The population growth among diverse people groups should challenge us to plant congregations that will reach the ever growing population in our midst.

HISPANIC POPULATION [123]

The Hispanic population continues to grow faster than the rest of its population. In the years between 2000 and 2002, it grew by 3.5 million to 38.8 million people.[124] Two factors contributed to the increase, a higher birth rate and high levels of immigration. The Hispanic population is very diverse, made up primarily of three distinct groups: Mexican, Puerto Rican and Cuban. Latinos of Mexican origin are more likely to live in the West (54.6 percent) and the South (34.3 percent); Puerto Ricans are more likely to live in the Northeast (58.0 percent); and Cubans are more highly concentrated in the South (75.1 percent). Central and South Americans were found in three regions: the Northeast (31.05 percent), the South (34.0 percent) and the West (29.9 percent).

The Hispanic population is about ten years younger (26 median age) than non-Hispanic Whites. Among Hispanics, Mexicans are the youngest with median age of 24 while the Cubans are oldest with median age of 43.

Hispanics have made positive strides in education. Slightly over five in ten have a high school diploma. This is an increase of six percentage points since 1989. Eleven percent held a bachelor's degree, which did not significantly change from a decade ago. One of the educational challenges for Hispanics is to reduce the 27 percent of the population that has less than a ninth grade education.

68 percent of Hispanic families are married couples. Another 25 percent are maintained by a woman with no husband present and are among the poorest. Mexican family households were most likely to have five or more people. Cuban family households were most likely to

have only two people. This statistic points to a younger Mexican-origin population where more than a third are under age 18.

The unemployment rate varies by group. The unemployment rate in 1994 ranged from a seven percent for Cubans to a high of fourteen percent for Puerto Ricans. The gender gap in earnings is smaller among Hispanics than non-Hispanics.

AFRICAN-AMERICAN POPULATION [125]

The Black population grew at a rate of 1.4 percent per year between 1980 and 1992. This is twice the annual growth rate of the White population (0.6 percent). Hispanics surpassed the Black population in the year 2000. Blacks are concentrated in the South (55 percent).

The Black population is younger than the non-Hispanic White population. More than a third of the Black population is under 18 years old. Like the young Mexican population, blacks are more likely to have five or more members in their household.

Fewer families contain a married couple. Such families comprised 56 percent in 1980 but only 48 percent in 2002. Consequently, during that same period, families maintained by women with no spouse present, rose from 40 percent to 43 percent. As a result, just 36 percent of Black children under 18 years old lived with both parents in 1992. Blacks were more likely to rent than to own a home in 1992 (56 percent versus 42 percent).

Blacks are closing the educational gap. In the twenty-two years between 1980-2002, Blacks aged 25 and over who had earned at least a high school diploma increased by 28 percentage points narrowing the gap to 79 percent versus 89 percent for Whites. Statistics clearly show that education does pay. The median earnings for a full time

Black worker aged 25 and over, who was a high school graduate, was $18,620, in 1991. But those with at least a bachelor's degree earned $30,910. However, Blacks still account for about one quarter of the population in poverty in 2001.

A S I A N   P O P U L A T I O N [126]

The Asian and Pacific Islander population is not a homogeneous group; rather it comprises many groups who differ in language, culture and length of residence in the United States. Some Asian groups, such as the Chinese and Japanese, have been in the United States for several generations. Others, such as the Hmong, Vietnamese, Laotians and Cambodians, are fairly recent immigrants.

One-half of the Asian and Pacific Islander population live in the West. It is possible that because the West coast is a gateway to the United States, it is easier for this population to remain in the West. Additionally, there is a long history of established Asian communities in the West that would make any transition less difficult.

Asian and Pacific Islanders live predominately in metropolitan cities. It is interesting to see the inversely proportionate relationship between people movements and the educational and income levels of the people. The percentage of Blacks living in central cities (52 percent) within metropolitan areas is larger than Hispanics (45.6 percent), which is larger than that of Asian and Pacific Islander (41 percent). In contrast, the educational and income levels of Asians are greater than that of Hispanics, which also is greater than that of Blacks.

This people group seems to have very stable marriages. The percentage of divorce of Asian and Pacific Islanders (5 percent) is half of non-Hispanic Whites. Because of the stability of the marriages, the majority of

Asian and Pacific Islander households are family households. In fact, of all the groups mentioned in this chapter, including non-Hispanic White, the Asian and Pacific Islanders have the lowest percentage of nonfamily households (27 percent).

A substantial difference existed in the level of higher education attained by Asian and Pacific Islanders and non-Hispanic Whites. Asian men were more likely to have earned at least a bachelor's degree than non-Hispanic Whites, a difference of nineteen percentage points. Asian women were more likely to have earned at least a bachelor's degree than non-Hispanic White women, a difference of seventeen percentage points.

AMERICAN INDIAN POPULATION [127]

Five million Native Americans and First Nations people live in the Unites States and Canada. Of these, ninety-five percent have yet to accept Christ.[128]

Four out of ten American Indians lived in the West. Additionally, five of the top ten cities with the largest American Indian populations were in the West; Los Angeles, Phoenix, San Diego, Anchorage and Albuquerque. The places with the largest American Indian population, however, were New York and Los Angeles with 87,241 and 53,092 respectively. According to Census 2000, the American Indian tribal groupings with 100,000 or more people were Cherokee, Navajo, Latin American Indian,[129] Choctaw, Sioux and Chippewa.

IMPLICATIONS FOR CHURCH PLANTING

The groups described above represent a very small part of four major classifications of language groups which comprise 33.1 percent of the United States population. Can you imagine how many nations one could influence with the gospel by reaching out to these groups? There are various implications for us to consider.

A biblical implication

The great commission (Matt. 28:19-20; Luke 24:47-49) challenges every believer to "Go and make disciples of all the nations." Many people have confused the term "nations" with countries in the world. I believe that the term "nations" speaks of people groups rather than individual countries. The emphasis of Acts 1:8 has been primarily on geography instead of the ethnolinguistic groups. For us to focus only on our own kind of people could be seen by God as the same departure that the Jews and the disciples allowed to occur as they withdrew from the Samaritans.

A cultural implication

God told the first couple to "be fruitful and multiply" (Gen. 1:22). As their family grew, they decided to build a large tower and a city in which they could protect their society. Many explanations have been presented to explain this action. Some have said it was an attempt at unity without God; a city of refuge in case of another flood; or as the first public statement on humanism "let us make for ourselves a name" (Gen 11:4). Whatever the reasons, these people were fearful of being "scattered abroad over the face of the whole earth" (Gen. 11:4), although they knew that it was a mandate from God to, "Be fruitful and multiply and fill the earth" (Gen.1:28). This group had one language and unity without God as a purpose, but God brought division. In Acts 2, there were people of many cultures and languages on the day of Pentecost, but the Holy Spirit brought everyone together and, "each one of them was hearing them speak in his own language"

(Acts 2:6). One may live geographically close to a person, yet you may be miles apart culturally. People want to hear the gospel in their heart language and in the context of their own cultural background.

A demographical implication

Demographical material can give a clear picture of the type of people that live in a specific area and provide other helpful information as well. A church planter should be very familiar with the people he/she is trying to reach before a strategic plan is created. The demographical material can be one helpful instrument that the church planter can use to develop a profile of the people to be reached.

An evangelistic implication

Ralph Winter's brilliant contribution to missiology was his identification of four kinds of evangelism. In order to impact the American mosaic, one must consider the evangelistic implication to church planting.

1. E-0 evangelism aims to renew existing Christians. Most of our ministry is directed to the marginal Christians who have no desire to evangelize.

2. E-1 evangelism is near-neighbor evangelism of non-Christians whose language and customs are those of the Christian who is witnessing.

3. E-2 evangelism is across a small ethnic, cultural, or linguistic gap.

4. E-3 evangelism across a large linguistic, cultural and ethnic chasm.

The demographical information coupled with the biblical implications ought to lead the church planter to examine the basis of his/her evangelism. We should share the gospel, not only with "our kind" of people, but with others that may be at some cultural, linguistic and ethnic distance from us. Keep in mind, that before you do E-2 and E-3 evangelism, you need to deculturize, feel at home in another culture and build bridges to the many segments of society where very few have become Christians.

A church growth implication

Every healthy congregation should be involved in four types of church growth.

1. Internal Growth is growth among sub-groups within the existing church. An example is the movement of marginal Christians to passionate belief.

2. Expansion Growth is increasing in numbers by conversion growth and adding them to the congregation. This is critical to the healthy growth and future reproduction of the church.

3. Extension Growth is the intentional planting of another congregation. This may be among "our kind" of people or across a distant cultural, ethnic and linguistic people group.

4. Bridging Growth is finding bridges to other segments of the population and, crossing the bridges of God, multiplying groups of the committed on the other side. An example of bridging growth is a congregation that intentionally reaches out to a singles group that is not been reached.

The regrettable condition of many congregations in North America today is that their inward focus has fully anesthetized them. They have neglected to feel the real needs of the people in their Jerusalem, Judea, Samaria and to the ends of the earth. Healthy reproducible congregations should have a well balanced approach to these four types of church growth.

CONCLUSION

What if . . .

1. A congregation is intentional about reaching a world for Christ?

2. A congregation is intentional about training people to evangelize individuals of different ethnic, cultural and linguistic backgrounds?

3. A congregation is intentional about starting church planting centers?

I believe that the result would be a rapid multiplication of leaders and congregations as well. Think of the many different cultures one could reach just in North America with our diverse population.

REFLECTION

1. Do a demographical study of your neighborhood (5-10 mile radius) and paint a picture of the American mosaic there. Who is your neighbor? What churches are reaching these groups? Could your church minister to any of these groups in your neighborhood? What is the social condition of the area?

2. Is there a concentration of Hispanics in your area? Where are they from? Why are they living in that area (employment, family, school, etc)? What type of ministries could be initiated in order to reach Hispanics in your area?

3. Where is the concentration of African-Americans in your area? What is their socio-economic background? Is there a church ministering to the African-American community?

4. Is there a concentration of Asians in your area? Where are they from? Why are they living in that area (employment, family, school, etc)? What type of ministries could be initiated in order to reach Asians in your area? Is there a church that ministers to Asians in the area?

5. Is there a concentration of American Indians in your area? What group do they represent? Why are they living in that area (employment, family, school, tribe, etc)? What type of ministries could be initiated in order to reach American Indians in your area? Is there a church that ministers to American Indians in the area?

6. What are the Biblical, cultural, demographical, evangelistic and church planting implications?

Elements of Indigenous Congregations

So the churches were being strengthened in the faith and were increasing in number daily (Acts 16:5).

Indigenous is something that is native to a particular place. For example, native shrubs such as Apache plume and Junipers are indigenous to New Mexico. All across the nation, communities faced with increased demands on existing water supplies are encouraging, and in some instances, mandating lawn and garden strategies aimed at conserving water. In 1994, the City of Albuquerque, New Mexico, launched a major water conservation effort to promote drought-hardy landscapes. However, acceptance has been slow since many of the people living in Albuquerque are transplants from parts of the country where it's a lot greener.[130] Herein lie the struggles between that which is indigenous and that which is foreign to a place.

The "Coquí" frogs are indigenous to Puerto Rico. These frogs are small, about the size of a quarter. Biologically they are of interest in that they are born as a frog instead of as tadpole. The coquí tends to stay in one area unless moved elsewhere by people.

An indigenous church is a contextualized church. It is able to grow within the culture where it finds itself, without any external control. Many have argued for and against the indigenous church principles. The purpose of this chapter is not to fan the flames of disagreement, but instead to present some elements found in the indigenous church.

Indigenous church principles have theological and ecclesiological overtones. An indigenous church ought to reflect the culture of that land or region and not the culture of the missionary. Churches ministering to a particular language/cultural group need to mirror that group. It is counterproductive to attempt to anglicize a language congregation. The strength of that congregation is in the people, their culture and the way they worship the Lord. The emphasis should be in lifestyle changes from the old life to a new life rather than a change from their cultural backgrounds to the culture of the missionary who is evangelizing them.

John L. Nevius, a Presbyterian missionary serving in China, wrote, "Planting and Development of Missionary Churches," a book that has become a missiological masterpiece. This book developed out of two weeks of lectures to young Korean pastors just starting their ministries. Nevius' call for an indigenous church states what may very well be one of the most influential mission methods ever written. In his book, Nevius describes the indigenous method under six principles.[131]

First, he strongly believed that each convert "should remain in the situation where he was when God called him" (1 Co. 7:20). In other words, each person continues to earn his living just as he did before he became a Christian and to live in the same place where he lived before he was baptized. Second, trust unpaid lay leaders to shepherd the flock. These are unpaid leaders that develop from within the congregation. Third, the church should meet in the homes of the members. Fourth, the churches should be supervised by paid evangelists or helpers and by the missionary himself. Nevius strongly believed in mentoring others as they developed indigenous congregations. "It is our aim that each man, woman and child shall be both a learner from some one more advanced and a teacher of some one less advanced."[132] He was responsible, as the missionary, for supervising 10 churches as well as overseeing the entire work of sixty churches. One of his helpers supervised forty churches and another, ten churches. These helpers visited each of the churches regularly once every two months. The helper normally stayed in each place for a week. On Sunday, the helper modeled for the pastors and leaders the pattern to follow in their several congregations during the seven to eight weeks they are by themselves. Fifth, provide extensive training to members. Sixth, new churches are planted by existing congregations. These churches naturally multiply through the existing web of relationships.

There are some concepts and theological positions that may bring excess baggage to planting indigenous congregations.[133]

1. The idea that a church, which meets in a church building is more genuine than a church that meets in a home.

2. A flawed definition of what a church is.

3. The idea that only the professional clergy can be effective church planters.

4. Low expectation level for new believers.

5. The idea that if a church ceases to function as a group, the church planter is a failure.

These reasons have a snowball effect in the way we look at church planting. Many people associate the church with a building instead of the people of God. This is neither biblical nor practical. Of course, this mindset is the product of misunderstanding of what the church is. It is also a factor in the growing chasm between clergy and laity. These five reasons become insignificant when put side by side with the Word of God. The lowest common denominators are people and the Word.

The church was defined in chapter four as "a group of called and baptized believers that gathers together regularly for evangelism, ministry, fellowship, worship and prayer" (Acts 2:42-47). The church is not a building, but the people of God. The church is not dependent on where people meet to worship.

The goal of the church planter is to start healthy reproducible congregations indigenous to that particular region and exhibiting the three characteristics of the New Testament church: self-governing, self-supporting and self-propagating.

The principle of self-governing is very important to local congregations. Scripture teaches that each congregation is to be Christ-centered. We must make a distinction between a democratically-run church and a Christ-centered church. In the former, people are free to express their voices and desires. However, the latter, puts Christ as the supreme authority in all decision-making, despite our desires. From its inception, the new congregation ought to be self-governing. Many ask how they can govern themselves without sufficient knowledge and experience to make decisions. It is true that a new congregation may not be as knowledgeable or have the experiences of a more mature congregation; even so, they need to make their own decisions. This is part of normal healthy growth. When the flames of self-governing are suppressed, self-supporting and self-propagating will be destroyed and the congregation will cease to be indigenous. This is not to say that the role of the missionary is a silent one. To the contrary, he should give advice and direction to the leadership, being careful that he does not make the decisions for the group.

The principle of self-support teaches that a new congregation must sustain itself from the beginning. Of the three characteristics, this is perhaps the most difficult one to accept. Many have argued that no congregation can possibly be self-supporting from the start. Proponents of the indigenous principle maintain that if a congregation is truly indigenous from its inception, they will accomplish only the things they are able to do with their available finances. Ideally, a new congregation has all the needed financial resources to conduct its basic ministries. Donald McGavran expressed some fear that this model would become an idol. McGavran adds:

Indigenous church principles work well where many are won soon, but are not effective where few are. Nevius's thousand converts came rapidly in a rural population where large famine relief had been distributed in the previous decade. The movement to Christ created sixty churches in a short time. St. Paul also went to synagogue communities where congregations were rapidly established. Had he been evangelizing resistant populations, where converts were gathered one by one over many years and churches arose from these occasional converts, famine orphans, rescued persons and converted schoolchildren, would he have been able to depend on an unpaid local leadership?[134]

Kingdom principles call for an understanding of how these useful tools can be used to disciple a nation. Because mankind is so diverse, it is important to look at the things that can bring us together rather than those that separate us into two different camps. Some suggestions that may help reconcile these two conflicting positions are:[135]

1. The goal of evangelistic churches is independent congregations and the first [church plant]one ought to be planted according to indigenous principles. These are much wider in scope than the limited question regarding support.

2. When planting congregations in an area where older churches are growing and not subsidizing pastors; do not provide support to the new churches.

3. If new congregations are growing without a paid pastor, do not start new ones with subsidy

4. When starting new congregations in areas where previous churches are receiving financial support, there are three options:
   a. provide financial support
   b. start a new congregation forty to fifty miles away and seek to start without subsidy
   c. start congregations that minister to a totally different population

5. When starting a new congregation in resistant areas, try to start with indigenous principles. However, do not continue with the indigenous principles if it does not seem to work in that area. To continue would be bad stewardship of God's resources.

6. Financial help may be necessary at the beginning, but should not develop into dependency. No true growth will happen until the congregation is able to provide their own support.

7. Train unpaid leaders in all congregations even if the current pastor receives subsidy.

8. Work continually toward church multiplication.

9. Make provisions for paid leaders at the supervisory level. Sometimes it is best to establish a church fund from which pastors are paid.

The principle of self-propagation teaches that each healthy congregation should reproduce. This is the type of church that is evangelistic and has a passion to initiate new congregations as well. With the population growth we are experiencing, it is necessary that churches make a commitment to reproduce in order to reach the growing population.

It is regrettable that many of the present churches entered the 21st century only to realize that they are unprepared to minister to a growing and different world. Many of our churches today insist on ministering with methods used in the 1950's. Many others endeavor to reach this generation with new and different tools. In the midst of the rapid changes occurring in our society, it is the Word of God that remains unchanged. Peter reminded his generation of this truth "All flesh is like grass and all its glory is like flowers of the grass. The grass withers and the flowers fall off, but the word of the Lord endures forever" (1Pet. 1:24-25).

Do not let irrelevant arguments distract you from concentrating on the main task, which is to start healthy reproducible congregations. Fight weariness with the Word of God and distraction with discipline. Take a good look at your area of ministry and listen to the Lord say, "The harvest is plentiful, but the workers are few. Therefore beseech the Lord of the harvest to send out workers into his harvest" (Mt. 9:37-38). We indeed have a remarkable opportunity to make a lasting contribution by training leaders who will start healthy reproducible congregations in our Jerusalem, Judea, Samaria and to the ends of the earth.

REFLECTION
1. Research the ministry of John L. Nevius.

2. Describe an indigenous church.

3. What are some concepts and theological positions that may bring excess baggage to planting indigenous congregations?

4. Explain the principles of self-governing, self-support and self-propagating.

HAPTER *28* *Objections to Church Planting*

But seek first His kingdom and His righteousness, and all these things will be added to you (Mt. 6:33).

*C*harles was very upset at our church planting strategies. He came to my office wanting an explanation as to why we started a new congregation close to the one his church had started. I spent some time understanding his fears, concerns and the anger he demonstrated. After about two hours, we finished the meeting. While I do not think I answered all his questions; he said to me, "I don't agree with all you are doing in church planting, but I have to admit that good things are happening."

In the second chapter of this book, I mentioned that church planting is kingdom growth, is exciting and should be a joyful experience. But the other side of the same coin is that church planting is very controversial. Self-centeredness is at the core of this controversy. This self-centeredness may be momentarily camouflaged by elaborate arguments, but this position will not conceal the lack of support for Kingdom growth. In this chapter, I want to mention some objections I have heard, their rationale and the response to the objection.

Objection: "We have enough churches."

Rationale: There are enough churches in my area. We think is a waste of God's resources to start new churches

Response: The number of church buildings does not determine whether an area is churched. Rather, one needs to study the population to church ratio to determine if more churches are needed. Please see the reflection area in chapter three to determine the unchurched population in your area.

Objection: "We need to strengthen the struggling existing churches."

Rationale: I do not see the point of starting new congregations when many of the existing ones are struggling and dying.

Response: Certainly one shouldn't ignore struggling churches. However, investing time and monies for a long period of time in struggling congregations is not good stewardship. Persistently, these struggling congregations have not taken opportunities to reach out to a changing community, consequently they have declined in membership and become out of touch with that community. Therefore, it is more cost-effective, in terms of time, monies and evangelism, to start new congregations.

Objection: "My church is doing a good job of reaching the people in my community."

Rationale: We do not need to start a new congregation in this area since this church is doing a very good job at reaching the people in the community.

Response: We rejoice when any church thrives by reaching out to a lost group of people. With growing urban centers in the world as well as rural communities, no single church is able to reach out effectively to all segments of the population.

Objection: "I would like to start a new church, but the cost of land makes it almost prohibitive."

Rationale: In order to start a new church the "right way," we must purchase land for the new church.

Response: This statement makes the assumption that a new congregation must purchase land in order to be a church. This is an inadequate understanding of how Scripture defines church. It is difficult for a new congregation to purchase land from the start.

Objection: "We will lose members."

Rationale: If we start new churches, we will lose members and we simply cannot afford to lose anyone.

Response: This is a disappointing statement, not necessarily verbalized, but in the mind of many church leaders. This goes back to the heart of the problem, which is self- centeredness. My personal experience shows that churches which freely give members to start the core group of new congregations are blessed by God with new members to replace those serving in the new church.

Objection: "We are too small."

Rationale: We are not able to start a new congregation because we are too small and limited in resources.

Response: This presupposes that the small church is responsible for the church planting process. A small church may be part of church planting efforts by joining with other partner churches. They could do prayer walking, lead Bible studies, distribute evangelistic materials, provide limited financial resources, etc.

Objection: "It will drain our finances."

Rationale: Starting a new congregation will put a financial burden on our church.

Response: Starting a new congregation does not always involve finances. There are churches that can be started with very limited financial resources. Some may add that if you "give away" people you will also lose income. My personal experience is that God will supply all your needs. (See above objection: "we will lose members").

Objection: "It will split my church."
Rationale: Starting a new congregation will split my church by taking away members
Response: God expects every healthy organism to reproduce. The church, if it is a healthy organism, desires to reproduce. Remember that church planting is a process which takes time. If the pastor, through his leadership, provides teaching and communication to the membership about the opportunities for reaching people through a new church start, it will only create enthusiasm. Keep in mind that there are many things a congregation can do in order to start a church (see "we are too small").

Objection: "We need to strengthen our church first."
Rationale: Before we start a new congregation, ours must be strong.
Response: I have heard pastors of churches with five hundred members make this statement. The question one must ask is, "How big must a church be to become strong?" A church, which focuses her efforts on intentional missionary outreach, will not only grow in number, but in knowledge as well.

Those that support church planting should certainly not take a "we" and "them" position. Instead, try to understand and build a good relationship with the person who is expressing objections. Often these objections lessen with more understanding of biblical and practical principles of church planting.

The task of the church planter is to educate and effectively communicate the benefits of a new congregation. Building relationships will facilitate the transition from one who opposes, to one who is open to new congregations. It is the church planter's responsibility to initiate, maintain and break down any walls of division that may exist.

REFLECTION

1. Write an article (three to six paragraphs) describing your philosophies of church planting.

2. What are some objections to church planting you have heard? How would you respond to the objections?

3. What can you do to provide a solution to the objections?

One Final Word

Therefore if there is any encouragement in Christ, if there is any consolation of love, if there is any fellowship of the Spirit, if any affection and compassion, make my joy complete by being of the same mind, maintaining the same love, united in spirit, intent on one purpose (Phil. 2:1-2).

oel and DeeDee opened their home to a weekly Bible study. For months, we faithfully met at their home and learned what great love they had for our Lord. Some of the members of the partner church came to teach Scripture to the children. Others came to teach Bible studies to the adults. Others came only once to take pictures to display as a promotional piece at the partner church. Others supported the initial ministries with prayers. Different people had a small part of the entire church planting experience.

Months later this Bible study came to an end. Some in the group became part of the core group of the new congregation. Others felt led to continue serving in their own church. As this core group grew, additional members from the partner church came to be part of this core group and eventually, of the new congregation.

Each of us use our "connections" at work, church, with friends and in neighborhoods to invite people to the new church. Many of us connected with lost people and used the opportunity, not only to share Christ with them, but also to invite them to be part of the new church. Some had a small part, while others were able to invest more time in this effort. The valuable lesson one can learn from this story is that it takes different kinds of people and different types of ministries to start a church.

As we move toward the conclusion of this book, I trust that you have captured the picture of how essential it is to "connect" with one another if we are to have a positive influence in developing people and developing healthy reproducible churches. The premise for this book has been that only spiritually healthy people can start healthy reproducible congregations. Anyone interested in church planting must first connect to God before he can connect to others. Church planting is all about how people connect with one another, with the church and most importantly, with the Lord.

One of the most detrimental mistakes Christians make is to build walls that separate them from the unchurched world. The longer one is a Christian, the greater the chances of isolation. How then will the Christian become salt to a tasteless community? There are examples of connections in Scripture.

The apostle Paul was always connected to the community of his day. Whenever he visited a city that had a synagogue, he would visit there and preach the gospel. When he encountered the religious people at Athens, he stood up in the midst of the Areopagus and said,

Men of Athens, I observe that you are very religious in all respects. For while I was passing through and examining the objects of your worship, I also found an altar with this inscription, "TO AN UNKNOWN GOD." Therefore, what you worship in ignorance, this I proclaim to you (Acts 17:22-23).

The Lord Jesus saw beyond the deception of Matthew and the tempestuous character of Peter. As Matthew sat in the tax collector's booth, Jesus told him "Follow Me!" (Mt. 9:9). Peter and his brother Andrew were fishermen and while they were casting a net into the sea, Jesus said to them, "Follow Me and I will make you fishers of men" (Mt. 4:19).

The woman of Samaria was blinded by her religion and entangled in a life of sin. She had married five husbands and now was living with the sixth man. Jesus connected by meeting her physical and spiritual needs. But He also connected to many in the city of Samaria through her. "From that city, many of the Samaritans believed in Him because of the word of the woman who testified, 'He told me all the things that I have done,'" (Jn. 4:39).

Paul had a vision; "a man of Macedonia was standing and appealing to him and saying, 'Come over to Macedonia and help us'" (Acts 16:9). Paul was one of four missionaries in Philippi. He looked for a synagogue, as was his custom, but found none. There was a place of prayer outside the gates of the city where women used to gather and Paul went there to proclaim the gospel. There he divinely connected with Lydia, a worshiper of God. The Lord opened her heart and she and her household were baptized. She immediately opened her home to the missionaries. "If you have judged me to be faithful to the Lord, come into my house and stay" (Acts 16:15). But Lydia not only opened her home to the missionaries, she also opened her home to the entire community for a church. "They went out of the prison and entered the house of Lydia and when they saw the brethren, they encouraged them and departed" (Acts 16:40). This suggests a gathering of believers at Lydia's house-church. These are connections, some have a larger role than others, but all lead to reaching people for Christ.

What do you see as you look around your neighborhood? What do you hear the Lord telling you to do? What will your part be in connecting to others? What will be your task in reaching people for Christ?

ONE FINAL CHALLENGE

What if . . .

1. You made a commitment to open your home as Lydia did?

2. You made a commitment to prayer walk around an area in your city that needs a new church?

3. You made a commitment to lead a Bible study in your neighborhood?

4. You made a commitment to provide nursery care for a church in its beginning stages?

5. You made a commitment to intentionally pray for new workers, new churches and new believers?

6. Your church made a commitment to start one multiplying church every three years?

This chart shows the growth that would result if a church starts a church every three years and these churches also start churches every three years.

Chart 11

# Churches per Year		Yr 1	Yr 2	Yr 3	Yr 4	Yr 5	Yr 6
	1	1	1	2	2	2	4
	2	1	1	3	3	3	9
	3	1	1	4	4	4	16

The chart above shows, even with minute numbers, the exponential growth that can result when one uses the principle of multiplication. If a church starts only one church every three years there would be four congregations at the end of six years. Starting two churches every three years would more than double the number of churches in six years. Now observe the growth that occurs when a church starts three new churches every three years. The difference between a church starting one and three congregations every three years is twelve additional congregations or three hundred percent growth. Wow!

What will we need to make this multiplication become a reality?

1. A commitment to reach people for Christ (Connecting)

2. An understanding of the Biblical reasons for Church Planting (Word)

3. Identifying the place you have in Church Planting (Calling)

4. A motivation to be equipped (Equipping)

5. A readiness to be utilized (Mobilization)

6. Discovering a place where a new church is needed (Planting)

7. Committing to the principle of multiplication (Multiplication)

The explosive population, the degradation of the moral fibers of society and the sinfulness of mankind require that the people of God rise up and be counted.

The harvest is plentiful but the workers are few. Therefore beseech the Lord of the harvest to send out workers into His harvest (Mt. 9:37-38).

HOW WILL YOU RESPOND?

REFLECTION
1. Describe ways you are connecting with people. How many of these people are unchurched and/or lost?

2. What do you see and hear in your neighborhood? How could you minister to the needs in your community?

3. What role could you play in a new church planting experience? Are there any hindrances to your total surrender? How could you overcome the obstacles?

Multiplication

Practical steps I can take

1. Do an in-depth study of the book of Acts. Look carefully at Paul's methodologies for starting churches. Examine how:
   — He ministered to people groups
   — He used indigenous principles
   — He connected with people

2. As you work with the pastors of the new congregations started by your church; lead them to develop a profile of new areas where churches need to be started.
   — What types of churches are needed?
   — What type of people live in the area?
   — What is their educational background?
   — What is their religious background?
   — Do they attend a local church? Why or Why not?

3. Ask God to lead you to a person you could mentor.

4. Prepare a series of study/discussion type questions to lead the pastors of the congregations your church has started. Think of areas such as administration, theology, worship, evangelism and practical matters to name a few. You should allow time for functional team meetings. That is, worship leaders meet with worship leaders, administrators with administrators, etc. so that they can learn from each other.

About the Author

Dr. Gustavo V. Suárez was born in Havana, Cuba. He and his parents left Cuba in 1963 in search of political freedom. His journey took him to Panama, Nicaragua, Colombia, Chile and the United States.

Dr. Suárez' cross-cultural experience makes him uniquely qualified to minister in a multicultural world. He has experience in both rural and urban areas and has ministered both on the East and West coasts of the United States. He has been involved in church planting for more than two decades in Tennessee, New York, Maryland and New Mexico. He has led conferences for church planters throughout the United States.

Dr. Suárez received his Bachelor of Science degree from the University of Maryland, College Park, Master of Divinity degree from Mid-America Baptist Theological Seminary and the Doctor of Ministry degree from Golden Gate Baptist Theological Seminary.

Dr. Suárez and his wife Diana, a surgical nurse, have two children, Phillip and Matthew. They live in Albuquerque, New Mexico.

Conferences by the Author

Dr. Suárez is available to lead these conferences in English and Spanish.

Title: *Connections*
Content: This conference gives an overview to church planters, staff and lay people who want to build strong churches. This is a study of the six principles for dynamic church multiplication. The book, Connections: Linking People and Principles for Dynamic Church Multiplication will be discussed.
Time: 6 hours

Title: *Supervision*
Content: This workshop examines the definition of supervision and special emphasis is given to the development of a covenant, elements of supervision and the supervisory process which includes the stages and states of supervision.
Time: 18 hours

Title: *Visionary Planning*
Content: It is planning process to help a local church develop a ministry plan. It guides the local congregation to study who they are as a church, who is their neighbor, what are the ministry opportunities that will match the needs of the community and how to resource the plan.
Time: Start on Friday with Supper to Saturday at 3pm.

Title: *Fearfully and Wonderfully Made*
Content: Most problems are simple "people problems." They are misunderstandings of how people think, feel

and act the way they do. In this workshop, participants will take and discuss their personality and spiritual gifts profile. The uniqueness of this workshop is the combining and exploration of both the personality and spiritual gifts profile. Participants will also learn how they can use this tool in the churches to more effectively match people with ministry.

Time: Minimum of three hours.

Title: *Nehemiah: A Visionary Plan for Today*
Content: The uniqueness of this workshop is that it draws from the biblical teaching from the book of Nehemiah and makes practical application to a Visionary planning process that can be implemented in any local congregation or missionary strategy.

Time: One to Four Hours depending on schedule

Title: *Help me! I think I'm in Burnout*
Content: Explore the role of stress in burnout and how it affects our entire body – physical, emotional and spiritual areas. We will investigate helpful strategies to prevent burnout.

Time: 1–2 hours

End Notes

Introduction

1   A stage of development in a young person's life in the studies of communist doctrine.

2   Those guidelines were later changed by the mission board.

Chapter Two

3   Roland Allen, *Missionary Methods: St. Paul's or Ours?* (Grand Rapids: Wm. B. Eerdmans, 1979), 3.

4   C. Peter Wagner, *Church Planting for a Greater Harvest*, (Ventura: Regal), 11.

5   Donald McGavran, *The Bridges of God* (New York: Friendship Press, 1955), Introduction.

Chapter Three

6   Paul A. Beals, *A People for His Name: A Church-Based Missions Strategy* (Grand Rapids: Baker Book House, 1988), 11.

7   Aubrey Malphurs, *Planting Growing Churches for the 21st Century*, (Grand Rapids: Baker Book House, 2001), 35.

8   Malphurs, 37.

9   Ibid.

10   Ibid.

11   Eddie Gibbs, *Church Next: Quantum Changes in How We Do Ministry*, (Downers Grove: InterVarsity Press, 2000), 17.

12   An unevangelized continent is one which is lacking a multiplying movement of churches that could significantly impact major sections of that continent for Jesus Christ.

13   Malphurs, 44.

14   Daniel Sánchez, Ebbie Smith and Curtis Watke, *Reproducing Congregations: A Guide for Contextual New Church Development* (Cumming: Church Starting Network, 2001), 16.

Chapter Four

15   T.V. Farris, *Mighty to Save: A Study in Old Testament Soteriology* (Nashville: Broadman Press, 1993), 28.

16   Robert B. Girdlestone, *Synonyms of the Old Testament: Their Bearing on Christian Doctrine* (Grand Rapid: William B. Eerdsman Publishing Company, 1987), 76-77.

17   Darrell W. Robinson, *The Doctrine of Salvation* (Nashville: Convention Press, 1992), 10.

18   Girdlestone, 78-82.

19 Kenneth A. Matthews, *Genesis 1-11:26, The New American Commentary,* ed. E. Ray Clendenen, vol. 1a, (Nashville: Broadman & Holman Publishers, 1996), 239.

20 Farris, 39.

21 John Eadie, *A Commentary on the Greek Text of the Epistle of Paul to the Ephesians, The John Eadie Greek Text Commentary,* ed. W. Young, vol. 2, (Grand Rapids: Baker Book House, 1979), 167.

22 Robinson, 13.

23 Herbert Lockyer, *All the Parables of the Bible* (Grand Rapids: Zondervan Publishing House, 1963), 281.

24 Lockyer, 281.

25 Hershel H. Hobbs, *Romans* (Waco: Word Books, 1977), 42-43.

26 Robert H. Mounce, *Romans, The New American Commentary,* ed. E. Ray Clendenen, vol. 27, (Nashville: Broadman & Holman, 1995), 109.

27 Guy Greenfield, *We Need Each Other* (Grand Rapids: Baker Book House, 1984), 16.

28 Ibid.

29 Ibid, 102.

30 Ibid.

31 Bert Dominy, *Layman's Library of Christian Doctrine: God's Work of Salvation,* vol. 8 (Nashville: Broadman Press, 1986), 15.

32 Ibid, 17.

33 Greenfield, 128.

34 Jay E. Adams, *How to Help People Change* (Michigan: Zondervan Publishin House, 1986), 4.

35 David Keirsey and Marilyn Bates, *Please Understand Me* (California: Prometheus Nemesis Book Company, 1984), 2.

36 Oscar I. Romo, *American Mosaic: Church Planting in Ethnic America* (Nashville: Broadman, 1993), 16.

37 Gerhard von Rad, *Genesis: A Commentary,* trans. John H. Marks (Louisville: Westminster Press, 1961), 148.

38 Peter Wagner, *Spreading the Fire: A New Look at Acts—God's Training Manual for Every Christian, The Acts of the Holy Spirit Series* (Ventura: Regal Books, 1994), 87.

39 John B. Polhill, *Acts, The New American Commentary,* ed. David S. Dockery, vol. 26, (Nashville: Broadman Press, 1992), 176.

40 Ibid., 179.

41 Harvie M. Conn, ed., *Reaching the Unchurched: The Old-New Challenge* (Grand Rapids: Baker Book House, 1984), 26.

42 Ibid.

43 Archibald Thomas Robertson, *Word Pictures in the New Testament, vol. 4, The Espistles of Paul* (Grand Rapids: Baker Book House, 1931), 299.

44 Ibid.

45 R.C.H. Lenski, *The Interpretation of St. Paul's Epistle to the Galatians, to the Ephesians and to the Phillipians* (St. Paul: Lutheran Book Concern, 1937; reprint, Minneapolis: Augsburg Publishing House, 1961), 189.

46 Timothy George, Galatians, *The New American Commentary* ed. E. Ray Clendenen, vol. 30, (Nashville: Broadman & Holman Publishers, 1994), 289.

47 R.C.H. Lenski, *The Interpretation of St. Paul's Epistles to the Colossians, to the Thessalonians, to Timothy, to Titus and to Philemon* (St. Paul: Lutheran Book Concern, 1937, reprint, Minneapolis: Augsburg Publishing House, 1961), 166.

48 Ibid., 162.

49 Marvin R. Vincent, *Word Studies in the New Testament, vol. 3, The Epistle of Paul to the Colossians* (New York: Charles Scribner's Sons, 1887, reprint, Grand Rapids: William B. Eerdmans, 1977), 503.

50 Lenski, *The Epistle to the Colossians*, 163.

51 Lenski, *The Epistle to the Ephesians*, 439.

52 Jesse C. Fletcher, *The Mission of the Church, vol. 14, Layman's Library of Christian Doctrine* (Nashville: Broadman Press, 1988), 24-25.

53 John D. Floyd, "God's People—A Mission People," Mid-America Theological Journal 10 (Fall 1986), 3.

54 Levonn D. Brown, *The Life of the Church, vol. 13, Layman's Library of Christian Doctrine* (Nashville: Broadman Press, 1987), 53.

55 Ibid.

56 Bill J. Leonard, *The Nature of the Church, vol.12, Layman's Library of Christian Doctrine* (Nashville: Broadman Press, 1986), 90.

57 W.E. Vines, *Expository Dictionary of the New Testament Words* (New Jersey: Fleming H. Revell Comapany, 1940; reprint, New Jersey: Fleming H. Revell Company, 1966), 72.

Chapter Five

58 Beals, 13.

59 Sherwood G. Lingenfelter and Marvin K. Mayers, *Ministering Cross-Culturally* (Grand Rapids: Baker Book House, 1986), 11.

60 Edward Pentecost, *Issues in Missiology: An Introduction* (Grand Rapids: Baker Book House, 1982), 87.

61 Ibid., 88.

62 Paul G. Hiebert, *Antrhopological Insights for Missionaries* (Grand Rapids: Baker Book House, 1985), 53.

63 Ibid., 56.

64 Pentecost, 79.

65 David J. Hesselgrave, *Communicating Christ Cross-Culturally* (Grand Rapids: Zondervan Publishing House, 1978), 97.

66 Pentecost, 94.

67 Hiebert, 129.

68 Lingenfelter amd Mayers, 45.

69 Jung Young Lee, *Marginality: The Key to Multicultural Theology* (Minneapolis: Fortress Press, 1995), 40-41.

70 Susan E. Keefe and Amado M. Padilla, *Chicano Ethnicity* (Albuquerque: University of New Mexico Press, 1987), 46-51.
71 Keefe and Padilla, 42.
72 Ibid.

Chapter Six

73 Delos Miles, *Church Growth: A Mighty River* (Nashville: Broadman Press, 1981), 96.
74 Ebie C. Smith, *Balanced Church Growth: Church Growth Based on the Model of Servanthood,* (Nashville: Broadman Press, 1984), 51.
75 Ibid., 52.
76 Pentecost, 163-167.
77 Smith, 59-60
78 Ibid., 57.
79 Miles, 99.
80 Kent R. Hunter, *Foundations for Church Growth: Biblical Basis for the Local Church* (Corunna, Indiana: Church Growth Center, 1994), 86.
81 Conn, 121.

Chapter Seven

82 Malphurs, 89.
83 Charles Ridley, *How to Select Church Planters,* (Pasadena: Fuller Evangelistic Association, 1988), 7-11.
84 In 1997 the Southern Baptist Convention formed the North American Mission Board.

Chapter Eight

85 Malphurs, 285.
86 Malphurs, 103.

Chapter Nine

87 Malphurs, 153.

Chapter Ten

88 Robert E. Coleman, *The Master Plan of Evangelism,* (New Jersey: Fleming H. Revell Company, 1978).
89 Ibid., 34.
90 These eight keys are adapted from Coleman's principles.

Chapter Eleven

91 Statistics from the Uniform Church Letter and Annual Church Profile, LifeWay Christian Resource, Nashville, Tenn; compiled by Research Services, North American Mission Board, Alpharetta, Ga.

Chapter Thirteen
92   Malphurs, 231.
93   Malphurs, 239.

Chapter Fourteen
94   *Multiplying Church Network Facilitator Manual*, (Alpharetta, Georgia: North American Mission Board, 2002), 93-94.
95   The terminology used here is an adaptation from Don F. Mabry, "What Kind of Sponsoring Church are You?" Louisiana Baptist Convention, Alexandria, Louisiana.
96   *Multiplying Church Network Facilitator Manual*, 88-90.

Chapter Seventeen
97   Source: Information from First View by Percept Group, Inc.

Chapter Twenty
98   Malphurs, 264.
99   James M. Kouzes and Barry Z. Posner, *Leadership Challenge*, (San Francisco: Josey-Bass Publishers, 1987) 98.
100 "Basic Training for Church Planter," Facilitator's Manual, (Alpharetta: North American Mission Board, 2001) 3-4.
101 These series of questions in the vision, values, mission, church system design and strategic planning sections are part of activities used during the Basic Training for Church Planters. I have adapted these for training I have conducted dealing with visionary planning.

Chapter Twenty-One
102 Joanne Keating, "What's in a Name," www.canadianparents.com.

Chapter Twenty-Two
103 The Church Planting Management System (CPMS) is an excellent tool that can help new or established congregations keep track of visitors as well as the developmental progress of the membership. This is a product of the North American Mission Board (NAMB).

Chapter Twenty-Three
104 I am using *disciple* as one who follows Christ and mentors another person.
105 Mike Regele and Mark Schulz, "10 Best Practices of a Robust Congregational Development Effort," Percept Group, Inc., 2003.
106 Ibid., 4.
107 The Ten Best Practices of a Robust Congregational Development Effort were: Growing commitment, Strategic plan, Specific targets or goals, Measurable actions, Integrated planning, Capable leadership, Demographic analysis, Financial support, Designated staff and Committee preparation.

108 Stephen A. Macchia, *Becoming a Healthy Church: 10 Characteristics*, (Grand Rapids: Baker Book House, 1999), 23.
109 Christian A. Schwarz, *Natural Church Development: A Guide to Eight Essential Qualities of Healthy Churches*, (Carol Stream, IL: ChurchSmart Resources, 1996), 42.

Chapter Twenty-Four
110 Kouzes and Posner, 16.
111 Christian A. Schwarz and Christoph Schalk, *Implementation Guide to Natural Church Development*, (St.Charles, IL: ChurchSmart Resources, 1998), 137.

Chapter Twenty-Five
112 Hellenist were Greek speaking Jews.
113 C. Peter Wagner, *Lighting the World*, (Ventura, California: Regal Books, 1995), 99.
114 Ibid., 152.
115 Ibid., 146.
116 John B. Polhill, *The American Commentary: Acts*, (Nashville, Tennessee: Broadman Press, 1992), 269.
117 Ibid.
118 Wagner, *Lighting the World*, 162.

Chapter Twenty-Six
119 Source: from the North American Mission Board, Annie Armstrong promotion 2001.
120 Poem by Emma Lazarus at the Statue of Liberty.
121 Source: from the North American Mission Board, Annie Armstrong promotion 2001.
122 Source: U.S. Census Bureau, Population Profile of the United States: 2000.
123 Source: U.S. Census Bureau, The Hispanic Population in the United States, March 2002.
124 The Hispanic population of 38.8 million does not include Puerto Rico.
125 Source: U.S. Census Bureau, The Black Population in the United States, March 2002.
126 Source: U.S. Census Bureau, The Asian and Pacific Islander Population in the United States, March 2002.
127 Source: U.S. Census Bureau, The American Indian and Alaska Native Population: 2000.
128 On Mission, "Get Ready for your mission trip to native America, (NAMB, July-August, 2003).
129 In 1997, The Office of Management and Budget definition of American Indian or Alaska Native included the original peoples of North and South America (including Central America).

Chapter Twenty-Seven

130 Lana Robinson, "Landscaping with Native Plants," www.igin.com, May 2002.

131 Doanld A. McGavran, *Understanding Church Growth,* (Grand Rapids, Michigan: William B. Eerdmanns Publishing Co., 1980), 376-377.

132 John L.Nevius, *Planting and Development of Missionary Churches,* (Nutley, New Jersey: Presbyterian and Reformed Publishing Company, 1958), 32.

133 Charles Brock, *Indigenous Church Planter: A Practical Journey,* (Neosho, Missouri: Church Growth International, 1994), 40.

134 McGavran, 383.

135 Ibid., 384-385.